ate

From CIÉ to IR

The Changing Face of Ireland's Railways

From CIÉ to IR

The Changing Face of Ireland's Railways

Mark Darby, Neil Higson and Paul Quinlan

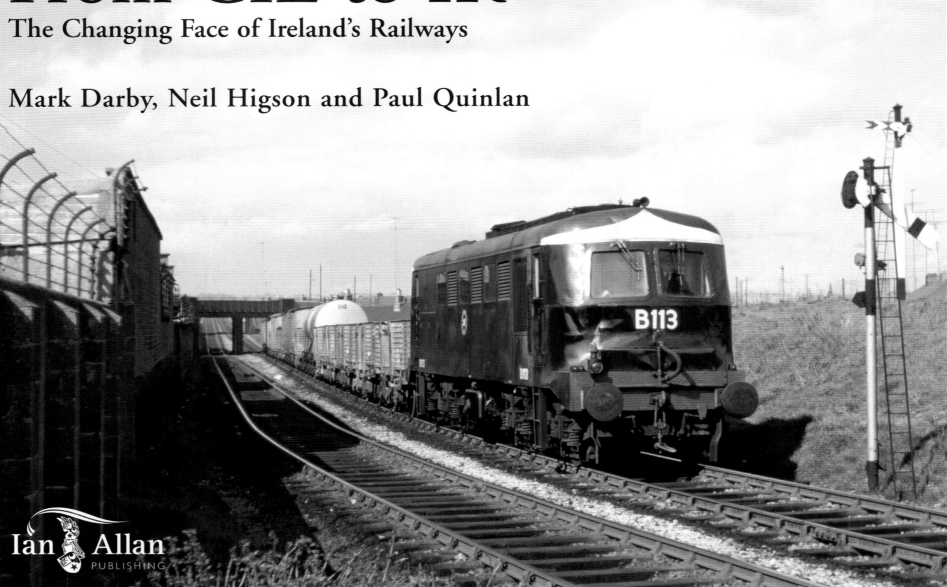

Ian Allan PUBLISHING

Front cover

No 167 threads the tunnels at Bray Head with the 09.35 Dublin to Rosslare service. Bray Head (Ceann Bré), County Wicklow, is now designated a Special Amenity area and is popular with walkers and birdwatchers, as the cliffs support a wide variety of breeding seabirds such as kittiwakes, cormorants, fulmars and various species of auk. *Antony Guppy*

Back cover

A little over ten years ago, Gaillimh retained the infrastructure enjoyed by all social historians and railway enthusiasts alike; unfortunately, technology progresses, bringing with it safer but less charismatic train protection. At a little before 21.00 on 27 September 1996, semaphores stand guard, protecting the entrance to Galway. This traditional train control had a further seven years remaining. To the casual observer colour light signals commenced control on 8 June 2003, wiping out the signal boxes at Ballinasloe, Athenry and Galway, with the ECP (emergency control panel) at Athlone assuming temporary command! Full CTC integration took place later in the year, on 30 November. *Mark Darby*

Title Page

Arguably the most influential locomotive ever to ply the Republic's metals was the first of the Inchicore Sulzer 'twins'. As No 1100, B113 holds the honour of being the country's first main-line diesel locomotive. Prior to the application of yellow warning panels, this fabulous shot from the camera of David Boyle depicts No B113 passing Ossory Road (known as "the dip"), between North Strand Junction and Church Road Junction, having just passed beneath the former GNR(I) main line, less then a mile out of Connolly station, with a transfer freight from Heuston Yard to North Wall, on 6 April 1968. *David Boyle*

From CIÉ to IR
Mark Darby, Neil Higson and Paul Quinlan

First published 2010

ISBN 978 0 7110 3476 1

Published by Ian Allan Publishing

an imprint of Ian Allan Publishing Ltd, Hersham, Surrey KT12 4RG.
Printed in England by Ian Allan Printing Ltd, Hersham, Surrey KT12 4RG.

Visit the Ian Allan Publishing website at www.ianallanpublishing.com
Distributed in the United States of America and Canada by BookMasters Distribution Services.

This book is dedicated to

PAUL ALEXANDER HIGGINS

1962–2009

"Fab fotter and taker of blurred Deltic pictures"

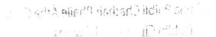

Introduction

A brief history of mixed-traffic diesel locomotives in the Republic of Ireland

The dawning of almost complete 'unitisation' spreading throughout Connaught, Munster and Leinster brings with it the realisation that the distinctive time-honoured cry of General Motors-powered locomotives, both 'Big' and 'Small', was, unfortunately, set to decline rather dramatically by 2010. *From CIÉ to IR* is a pictorial tribute to the Republic's mixed-traffic traction, as its swansong years approach a lamentable conclusion. The pictorial content contained within this album concentrates mainly on the previous 20 years, but with coverage of the majority of lines over which the main classes of diesel locomotives worked. We have employed a random geographical and loco-type approach, together with brief coverage of operations just over the border, in the north of the country, which we feel complements the aim of the book.

Córas Iompair Éireann (CIÉ) first took the decision to modernise, and as far back as 1946 the Board approved an order for its first two main-line diesel locomotives.

Early orders saw locomotives powered by Sulzer and Crossley engines, assembled by various contracted companies with subsequent orders built completely by General Motors at La Grange, Illinois, and latterly London, Ontario, in Canada.

The first diesel-powered mixed-traffic locomotive took to the charmingly time-warped and largely rural routes around the Republic of Ireland later than originally intended, early in 1950, lack of raw materials being the principal reason for the delay. The honour of the first main-line diesel locomotive to ply the Republic's metals fell to a rather diminutive 915hp Sulzer-powered Córas Iompair Éireann product, classified C2a, bearing the original number 1100, and out-shopped in green livery. Classmate No 1101 subsequently emerged, also from Inchicore Works, in October the following year. The C2as were the only CIÉ diesels to be fitted with a train-heating boiler, and thus required double manning; a 'fireman' was required to look after the boiler, which frequently tripped out in what was famously described as the 'arctic blizzard' conditions of the engine room that could prevail on a bitter winter's night!

Both 80-ton locomotives were initially diagrammed to various links on the main Cork artery from Dublin. In 1957 the pair were renumbered B113 and B114 respectively, and were notoriously unpleasant for the crew, having a negative reputation for intermittent, serious braking problems. The late 1960s saw the pair relegated to more mundane duties centred around Dublin. Their brake problems were ultimately 'the final nail in the coffin' for the pioneering Nos 113 and 114, both locomotives being out of traffic for several years awaiting brake system

This memorable image, taken in October 1978, depicts No 024 at the attractive market town of Youghal, which has been linked to the rail network since 21 May 1860. The 'A' has shunted her train of empty beet wagons and has marshalled the laden stock prior to the return trip to Cork. Youghal closed to passenger traffic on 2 February 1963, but popular Sunday excursions continued to run until the early 1980s, with up to three trains possible in a day! No 024 first took to the rails on 23 February 1956. *Richard Wall*

repairs prior to withdrawal. The axe finally fell on No 113 after working its final train back to Inchicore in January 1975. Although No 114 received modifications in 1974, it was destined never to turn a wheel again, and was laid to rest, ironically, at the Dublin birthplace of the 'twins'; April 1995 saw the scrap-man do his worst. No 113, however, received a cosmetic repaint in February 1996, but at the time of writing the locomotive is slowly rotting away. The pair survived long enough to carry black and tan, ending their days in CIÉ black with yellow warning panels, the early withdrawals precluding the application of any of the more startling garbs!

Subsequent builds

Five years were to elapse following the introduction of the pioneering Inchicore Sulzer 'twins' before, in July 1955, Dukinfield-built Metropolitan Vickers No A1, resplendent in a rather impractical silver livery and weighing 85 tons, became the 'new kid on the block'. The doyen 'A' became the first of an order totalling 94 locomotives from the Manchester company. The contract quoted two classes of motive power, consisting of 60 'As' and 34 lower-powered brethren in the shape of the 'C' class. As No C201 was not to debut until March 1957, we shall deal with the 'Cs' later, in their chronological order of introduction.

Powered by a Crossley 1,200hp engine, the iconic 'A' class had arrived. These locomotives were without doubt the most awesome pieces of modern-day traction, although only initially as far as their protagonists were concerned! The early days of service brought about disparaging remarks from passengers, such was the atmosphere of smoke and antisocial exhaust belched out by the new state-of-the-art Crossleys.

As with Nos 1100 and 1101, the 'As' were initially allocated to workings on the Cork route. Twelve months after the arrival of No A1, the 'Metrovick' revolution had spread to locations as diverse as the counties of Sligo and Wexford.

From May 1968 CIÉ initiated a re-engining programme, exchanging the unreliable Crossley HST V8 for the General Motors 12-645 E, rated at 1,325hp, the rebuild decreasing the weight, slightly, by 3 tons. No A58r was the first 'A' so treated.

It should be noted, however, that Nos 002, 027, 035, 036, 046, 056 and 059 received engines uprated to 1,650hp, together with traction motor rewinds and attention to the main generator, as they were intended for the CIÉ 'Enterprise'; subsequently, in their final years, these engines were either down-rated, or the locomotives were withdrawn. The programme to rebuild the 'Metrovicks' took 2½ years to complete, with No A26r the final member, released back into traffic late in 1971. From 1972 the class was gradually renumbered into its final number series, dropping the power classification prefix and rebuild suffix.

Rather paradoxically, following the power unit replacements, one of the present authors recalls an occasion in November 1994 when he was able to evocatively savour haulage behind oil-stained, work-worn No 039. After a sustained period of restricted running due to a succession of cautionary signals within a permanent way occupation south of Limerick Junction, No 039's driver eventually received the green signal. This was his cue to open the power controller with some gusto, and in a matter of moments sparks and small fireballs forged into an inky dark night sky, the display from the roof of the locomotive putting the opening ceremony of the Olympic Games to shame! The pyrotechnics attributed to the ignition of leaked oil collected within the silencer.

Terrorist activity

Over the years the troubles in the north of the country have been well documented, and several Metrovicks suffered a premature demise as a direct result of terrorism. The first 'A' to suffer withdrawal was No 008, which was blown up at Meigh on 23 October 1973. No 046 became the second class member to succumb when it was similarly bombed at Killeen Bridge on 21 April 1979. Three months later, on 23 July, No 004 was hijacked and set on fire at Goraghwood.

Writing on the wall

For many years the 001 class plied the length and breadth of the country, working all manner of trains as Ireland's premier front-line motive power, but the introduction of the 071 class in 1977

Doyen of the 1962 American-built 'Small' GMs, No 141 powers the 15.25 Waterford to Limerick stock delivery move on 1 May 2009. No 141, the oldest main-line loco still in IÉ operation at the time, had the job of delivering the newest piece of rolling stock, ICR outer suburban unit No 220042. This six-car unit was one of two delivered to the Port of Waterford a few days earlier from Korea, a long way from Tipperary where this photo was taken! With an order for 46 units (183 vehicles) worth approximately €400 million, Mitsui of Japan entered a partnership with Rotem of South Korea and the Tokyu Car Corporation of Japan to construct and deliver the three variants of this 100mph class. The beginning of the end for loco-hauled services began on 5 March 2007 when the MV *Chong-Ming* delivered the first four of the stainless-steel-bodied sets to Dublin. The class has achieved Iarnród Éireann's goal of removing all loco-hauled services from Ireland except for the services from Cork and Belfast to Dublin. In December 2008 a further order for another 51 vehicles was placed by the Irish Government, and speculation is that these will replace the locos and De Dietrich stock on the Belfast route. With 47 years between these two pieces of equipment, the tide of change on the Irish Rail system has certainly had an effect, and brings the story of diesel locomotives in Ireland full circle. *Neil Higson*

saw a gradual cascading to less glamorous diagrams. The mid-1980s saw a brief renaissance for the class on top-link duties as members of the 071 class passed through Inchicore Works for attention to frame fractures. The full introduction of the fleet of 201 'River' class locomotives, in the spring of 1995, was responsible for the final eradication of the 001s, the last three, Nos 003, 012 and 015, being retired in April 1995. Although officially withdrawn, No 003 hauled the Irish Traction Group's 'Flying Pig' railtour from Limerick to Limerick Check on 7 October, as at the time Limerick Wagon Works was the retired 'As' place of residence.

Enter BRCW

The second order for Sulzer-powered locomotives, which eventually became the B101 class, came about by a strange twist of fate. The Board of CIÉ placed an order in 1948 for six twin-engined 1,800hp express locomotives, again for services on the Cork line. Although work within contractors Vickers Armstrong and Metropolitan Vickers reached an advanced stage, change within the Irish Government led to attempts to cancel the locomotives. An alleged huge penalty clause upon cancellation caused much wrangling within the corridors of power at the Dáil, with the embryonic locomotives becoming very much a political 'hot potato'. After much discussion, the order for the express locomotives was cancelled, as recommended in the report by Sir James Milne. However, the equipment that had already been manufactured – the engines, by Vickers Armstrong (under a licence agreement with Sulzer), and the electrical equipment, by Metropolitan Vickers, could not be cancelled. It was delivered and stored at James's Quay, in Dublin, and initially CIÉ attempted to dispose of it. Instead, the result was the production of 12 mixed-traffic Birmingham Railway Carriage

& Wagon Company locomotives of 960hp, weighing in at 75 tons, which were assembled at BRCW's Smethwick factory. Enter the B101 class.

No B101 was taken into traffic in April 1956 and, like the Crossleys, painted silver. Unlike the Inchicore 'twins', the BRCW Sulzers immediately became favoured by their crews, offering superior comfort and, more to the point, a far better reliability than the Metrovicks. From 1958 they tended to work mainly on the Dublin-Waterford-Limerick-Cork axis, being frequently allocated to the Rosslare-Cork boat trains, together with goods services on the Waterford to Mallow line. Upon delivery of the B141s in 1962, they were relegated to hauling mainly goods traffic, and in their later years were confined to pilot, transfer and infrastructure duties. It is documented that No B106 had the honour of working the last train over the 'Burma Road', although some evidence suggests that stablemate No B103 may have ventured along the same line at a later date. No B111 suffered the ignominy of being the first class member to be withdrawn, in May 1969, due to fire damage. There was a proposal to extend the life of the BRCW 'Bs' with re-engining, but the arrival of the General Motors 071 class in 1977 scuppered that idea, and the final example, No 106, was withdrawn early in February 1978. Following the delivered silver livery came the application of green, and subsequently the black and tan and orange and black mixtures!

Metropolitan Vickers 'C' class

The concluding part of the order, from Dukinfield in Manchester, saw 34 550hp lightweight 58-ton Crossley EST V8-engined stablemates in the form of the C201 class (the locomotives' weight being increased by 4 tons upon final rebuild). Unlike their predecessors they were not intended for the Cork run, but for secondary routes and suburban traffic; however, many of their intended workings had already vanished by the time No C201 took to the rails in March 1957. Again, the livery was silver. As with the 'As', reliability of the Crossley engines became a bone of contention. General Motors was approached with regard to re-engining, and understandably was unimpressed with the prospect of matching its quality, reliable product with a locomotive type surrounded by such bad press. The first two 'C' class locos to receive transplants were Nos 234 and 233, being re-engined with Maybach MD-650 1,200hp units in December 1965 and May 1966 respectively at Inchicore. These power-plants, albeit with differing outputs and in pairs, were the same as those installed in all but one of the British Rail Class 42/43 'Warship' diesel-hydraulics. Although re-engined with the German diesel, CIÉ still desired the General Motors product for its Metrovick fleet, given the

superior reliability of the 52 Class 121 and 141 locomotives. A further order from the American company for 12 Class B181 locomotives in 1966 may have turned out to be a contributory factor to the La Grange outfit's change of heart over the supply of its power plants. The rebuilding of the 'Cs' with GM 8-645 E 1,100hp engines commenced with No 206 in September 1969, concluding with Nos 234 and 233 swapping their Maybachs in July 1979 and August 1980.

The 201-class locomotives will be fondly remembered for their push-pull work on the Dublin suburban trains, where they were the motive power for the de-engined and converted former AEC and Park Royal Class 2600 railcars, originally introduced between 1952 and 1954. The introduction of the Dart EMUs in 1984 put paid to these 30-year-old trains! At this point another of the present authors can confirm that if ever there was a train that showed how truly cash-starved CIÉ had become, it was the

As the original Crossley engines were proving to be unreliable, the entire fleet of Metropolitan Vickers 'A' and 'C' class locomotives subsequently passed through Inchicore to receive 'transplants'. The 'As' remained 'As'; however, upon receipt of more powerful 1,100hp engines the 'Cs' became 'Bs'! Photographed inside Inchicore in 1972, No C219 is undergoing rebuilding; she returned to traffic on 6 October as No B219. Withdrawal came on 25 September 1986, and scrapping followed four years later at the hands of Vic Berry. *Jonathan Allan*

The final vehicles in the order for 124 Mark 3 carriages emerged from Inchicore in 1988-9 as 19 push-pull intermediates and five control cars, intended for outer suburban use. From May 1994 a 121 class-powered three-piece set was based in Limerick, working between Ennis and Limerick Junction. One of the four class members to have had their rear windows over the bonnet removed during refurbishment, No 124 storms noisily away from the passing loop at Dromkeen with the 11.25 Limerick-Limerick Junction train on Sunday 23 March 2003. The other locos so treated were Nos 123, 131 and 134. This was the final regular passenger work for the class, ultimately being replaced by railcars on 9 March 2004. Freight and permanent-way trains continued to provide work for No 124 until it was withdrawn together with No 134 on 3 June 2008, bringing the curtain down on 47 years of hard work for the ground-breaking class. *Paul Quinlan*

push-pulls. He has a vivid recollection of a trip on the Bray to Greystones shuttle in 1984 when the trains were quite literally falling to bits. The seats had all been removed, and had been replaced by the multi-coloured stacking chairs one endured at school, dark and dingy – truly awful!

The first 'B' to suffer withdrawal was No 201, which, like three of the 'As', fell foul of terrorists, being bombed at Meigh on 15 August 1973. The majority of the class remained in service in the Republic through to the mid-1980s. The final three, Nos 213, 218 and 232, lasted until withdrawal on 24 November 1986, although No 213 remained active until February 1988, employed on pilot duties around Inchicore Works. Six class members, Nos 216, 218, 227, 228, 230 and 234, were sold to NIR in April 1986, and renumbered 104 to 109. Nos 104 and 108 (formerly 216 and 230) lasted until August 1995.

Some 201s suffered withdrawal twice! While the 071 class entered Inchicore Works for frame crack repairs, as well as the 'As' returning to front-line work at least nine 201s were temporarily resurrected to cover motive power shortages for up to eight months from April 1986.

Liveries carried by both classes of the former Crossleys progressed from the original silver through green, black, the addition of tan, and 'Supertrain', with various embellishments in between!

Step forward the 'Yanks'

Tired of poor reliability, CIÉ turned to America for help. The first product from La Grange, Illinois, was the 1960-built General Motors electromotive division (EMD) GL8 'switcher' design, which entered service in 1961. The locomotives were classified as the B121 class, weighed 64 tons, and were delivered in a more practical livery of grey and yellow. The production of the EMD GL8 designation ran to a build of 149 examples, although only 15 were destined for CIÉ, the remainder being exported to countries as far apart as Brazil and Bangladesh. The 'Yanks', as they were popularly known, commenced their careers, after various trials, working the 'enterprise', with B133 reaching Belfast on St Patrick's Day. They were responsible for the relegation of steam from the main line. In their fledgling years of service, trains would be hauled either cab or bonnet first; however, after an accident at Sallins, together with complaints from drivers regarding poor visibility when running bonnet first, it became compulsory to run with the cab end leading. This resulted in the retention of turntables at termini up and down the land. As the locomotives were not fitted for multiple-unit operation from new, it was not until the early 1970s, after the equipment had been retrospectively installed, that they could work in multiple with cabs facing outermost, or, later on, at the end of a push-pull set. The 121 class was immediately successful on passenger duties, but the locomotives' brakes were inadequate for loose-coupled goods, so they were normally restricted to passenger and fitted freight work. Experience led to the latter build of 'Small' GMs having upgraded braking from new. Liveries again included black and tan, and 'Supertrain' orange and black. The first class member to suffer withdrawal was No 125, back in March 1986, the result of an electrical fire. At the time of writing (autumn 2008) the final pair, Nos 124 and 134, had just been taken out of service, after almost 50 years of sterling work.

No competition

Taking into consideration the respect achieved by the 'Yanks' among the drivers, fitters and managers within the bastions of CIÉ, there was no competition whatsoever. When extra motive power became necessary, a further order for 37 locomotives was placed with General Motors in June 1962. Although similar in specification to the 121 class, the 141 class boasted a major operational advantage; the classification 'J' L8 denoted twin cabs, which was a landmark for EMD, being its first twin-cab design, as opposed to the 'G' L8, categorised by GM as the single-cab variety. The weight of the 141s was increased by 3 tons compared with their single-cabbed brethren. The new class featured further notable improvements, such as enhanced braking and the ability to operate in multiple with other class members, as well as 121-class locomotives, after they were retrofitted with multiple-unit equipment. The 950hp GM 8-567 CR power-plant was common to both types. All the 141s were delivered in the black and tan paint scheme.

The entire class were delivered and introduced into service within a couple of weeks of each other; the first examples, Nos 142, 150, 152, 155, 156 and 158, took to the rails on the same day, in the first week of December, only six months after the order had been placed! It is interesting to realise that, as they had been introduced rather en masse, major class examinations would fall due at the same time. It therefore became apparent that some kind of contingency plan would be required, and an edict was issued requiring individual locomotives to attain differing mileages. No problem! Even-numbered locomotives were assigned to high-mileage diagrams, with the odd-numbered examples receiving turns of lesser distances; the result was that the even-numbered locomotives passed routinely through the works first.

The Board of CIÉ, ambitious to make use of the higher outputs brought about by multiple operation of the 141s, set about initiating high-speed test runs, again on the 'premier' route to Cork, which were carried out through 1966. The accelerated timetable using pairs of 141-class locomotives began in June 1967. Since its introduction the class has worked almost every conceivable type of traffic, from crack express trains to station pilot duties. As time has progressed there have been many engine swaps between class members, with some 141s also receiving engines from defunct 201-class locomotives. The sole 'Small' GM to be honoured with a name was rather aptly No 150, which was christened *Inchicore Works 150 1846-1996* at the Works' 150th anniversary celebrations during the 15th of June 1996. Withdrawal of the class commenced in July 2002 with No 158, which had been stopped since March 1999.

Increases in passenger numbers, together with extra freight traffic and the declining reliability of a decrepit fleet of railcars, once again led to a call across the Atlantic Ocean. Early in 1966 CIÉ placed a further order for another 12 Bo-Bos along the lines of the 141s, and November saw delivery of the B181 class, with all locomotives placed into traffic by December of that year. The outward appearance of the class was almost identical to its 1962-built stablemates. The most obvious difference was the seven louvred vents under the headlight at either end, but beneath the hood or cowl lay the main change, an 8-645 E engine, delivering a higher 1,100hp output at no increase in locomotive weight. The reason behind the change was that General Motors had ceased production of its 567 series power-plant back in 1965. Like the 121 and 141 classes before them, the B181s were truly universal locomotives. The 141 and 181 classes were delivered in black and tan, subsequently receiving 'Supertrain' orange and black and Irish Rail's corporate colour scheme. No 191 became the first class member to suffer withdrawal, in April 1998, due to fire damage sustained during a runaway from North Wall in August 1991. Over the years CIÉ/IÉ has tended to be reluctant to introduce the scrap-man's oxyacetylene torch to its withdrawn locomotives, until recently; however, the famous Inchicore 'sound barrier' bears testimony to this former ethos!

The 'Big' GMs

After the arrival of the 181 class, almost a decade elapsed before, in 1975, the Board of CIÉ placed a further order with General Motors. The 18 locomotives of EMD's JT 22CW design were set to become not only the most powerful, delivering 2,450hp, but also the heaviest members of the Irish diesel fleet of the time, tipping the scales at almost 100 tons. The arrival of the 071 class signalled a short period of rather eclectic delivery patterns for the new Irish locomotive fleet. Upon completion in 1976, the La Grange-built 'Big' GMs were loaded onto barges and floated down the mighty Mississippi River as far as New Orleans, where the locomotive/barge 'combos' were transferred onto a huge ocean-going container ship, the 1973-built *Tillie Lykes*, for onward transit to the opposite side of the Atlantic. It was September and the Cold War was still in full swing, when the Lykes Line vessel anchored off Dublin Bay, her 39,000-ton displacement preventing entry into the Port of Dublin. It appears that one of the Eastern Bloc oligarchs of the time had confused the initials CIÉ with CIA, dispatching a 'spy' trawler to 'snoop' on the proceedings! Upon confirmation that the cargo was

nothing more sinister than motive power, the fishing-boat turned tail and headed for home – bigger fish to fry, perhaps?

Once the barges and their attendant hardware had arrived at the quayside, the 071s were offloaded and hoisted onto their waiting bogies. The locomotives were the first recipients of the 'Supertrain' livery from new, and their introduction was chequered, to say the least. During their first month on Irish metals, various familiarisation trips were undertaken until early October, when the proverbial large 'spanner' was thrown into the works, with the entire class being 'blacked' by the unions while a dispute over drivers' pay was resolved. The negotiations proved to be rather protracted, with the new locomotives lying idle in sidings around Inchicore depot. It was not until 23 May 1977 that No 082 became the first class member to turn a wheel in anger, hauling the 14.30 Heuston to Cork; services to Waterford and Galway quickly followed. As far as 'Achilles heels' went, the previously documented mid-1980s outbreak of frame fractures around the bogie pivots caused the most angst. Initially the locomotives also suffered from a poor ride quality. This problem was resolved by retrofitting them with yaw dampers as the locomotives passed through Inchicore for major overhauls from 1992 onwards. Until recently the 'Supertrain' livery, together with the subsequent addition of white lining and 'dayglo' orange warning panels, had seen the class through almost three decades of service. Only one class member has been named, No 082 becoming *The Institution of Engineers of Ireland* in a ceremony at Inchicore depot on 11 February 1997, in recognition of the body that was formed in 1835. In 2007 there was a radical shift at the Dublin works, as No 081 emerged supporting a shiny black and silver 'freight' livery – rather ironic, considering the scandalous current surrender of any non-passenger traffic by the incumbent railway leadership! At the time of writing all of the Republic's 'Big' GMs remained in service.

No 072 blasts away from Tullamore with the 17.10 Dublin to Athlone service on the evening of 30 April 2008. This regular 071 service was soon to become a push-pull set, which sadly meant the diagramming of a Class 201. The loco will be using all of its 2,250hp from its General Motors V12 EMD 12-645 E3C engine. The 645 series was available in a variety of sizes from a 1,500hp V8 up to the mighty 4,200hp V20. The 12-cylinder 45° Vee turbo-charged version in the 071s was introduced in 1968 and, in various forms, was fitted to more than 260 American-built engines such as the GP39/SD39, and Brazil's metre-gauge GT22 locos. In Europe Serbia ordered four ŽS series 666 locos, which were built to a similar outline as their Irish cousins in 1978.
Neil Higson

The 201 'River' class

Signed in November 1992, Iarnród Éireann's first and most probably only locomotive order was originally for 10 high-speed mixed-traffic diesel locomotives, subsequently increased to 32 with the help of additional European Union funding. The General Motors EMD classification, JT42HCW, had various designation codes common to other, smaller, stablemates, for example the 'J', which signified a twin-cab design. Weighing in at 112 tons and with 3,200hp available, the 201 class looks set to become the ultimate Irish Railways workhorse.

Without wishing to plagiarise any of the copy of the time (there was plenty), due to the nature of the arrival the delivery of the 201s was quite simply … spectacular. While the remainder of the class braved the more accepted method of transatlantic sea travel, No 201 sampled early life as a member of the 'jet set', travelling to Irish shores in the hold of UR 82066, a Ukrainian-registered Antonov 124. Minutes before 8 o'clock on the morning of 9 June 1994, the sleek new General Motors locomotive made history by becoming the heaviest load ever to land in Ireland, as the Russian-built monster touched down on the runway at Dublin Airport.

A departure from previous General Motors incarnations, the JT42HCW machines sprang from an alterative works; Canadian by birth, they were constructed at London, Ontario.

Class pioneer No 201 *Abhainn na Sionnainne/River Shannon* powers the 07.35 Waterford to Dublin Heuston service through County Kildare near Grange Beg on 8 August 2008. Its delivery 14 years earlier had made worldwide headlines as it arrived at Dublin Airport inside a huge 1992-built Antonov 124-100 (C/N 19530502761). With a 150-tonne payload capability, this former Russian military aircraft, then owned by Antonov Design (UR82066), was chosen so that Irish Rail could speed up the delivery process by starting driver training and clearance trials in advance of the production fleet, which came by sea. No 201 departed from London Airport, Ontario, at 13.15 on 8 June 1994, calling at Montreal, Gander and Reykjavik for fuel en route, landing at 07.40 on 9 June. Sadly in December 2008 the locomotive was stored at Inchicore, not required due to the downturn in loco-hauled diagrams in Ireland. *Mark Davies*

The pioneering Inchicore 'twins' aside, and in view of CIÉ's preference for generator vans, no further diesel locomotives built for the Republic's railways were equipped for train heating until the arrival of the 201s, which were fitted with head-end power (HEP); this supplies the train with all of its electrical requirements, for heating, lighting, air conditioning and cooking. Currently HEP is only used to power the De Dietrich stock used on the cross-border 'Enterprise' services. Upon ordering, Iarnród Éireann (IÉ) declined EMD's advice to install an auxiliary engine in the JT42HCW design to power HEP, which gives rise to situations such as the 12-cylinder engine sitting at Connolly station running at full power, as it must run at maximum rpm just to provide on-board electricity! One thing a diesel engine does not like is running at high revs per minute on a light load. The noise is quite phenomenal, and the fuel consumption awful, which gives rise to heavy general wear and tear. The 201s were also over-specified with ridiculous attributes such as dynamic brakes. These are handy holding back a 15,000-ton coal train on the gradients around the mountains of West Virginia, but completely unnecessary on the comparatively light trains and generally undemanding gradients of Ireland. It is doubtful if this equipment was ever commissioned.

The IR class members were delivered in a yellow and black livery, with a new corporate logo officially launched on 24 June 1994. A little over a month later, on 29 July, No 201 entered service on one of the Cork links. Nos 208 and 209 were subsequently delivered in blue livery, destined for Northern Ireland to be committed to the 'Enterprise' service. All locomotives were allocated the names of Irish rivers. Recent years have witnessed several livery changes, including the application of yellow ends, dedicated 'Enterprise' colours, and a green and silver 'InterCity' scheme to match the Spanish-built CAF Mark 4 carriage sets. As we prepared for press, the proverbial "wheel" had turned full circle, although incredibly the 30-year-old 071s still had a full complement of class members; the unprecedented, and totally unexpected rate of change within IR had condemned the newer non-Push-Pull equipped 201 (River Class) into "warm storage." Drained of fuel and lubricants, they were dumped unceremoniously, within the confines of Inchicore.

Principal services between Dublin, Cork and Belfast, albeit with differing stock and DVT's the remaining 201's final "Top Link" preserve.

Monday 21 September 2009 lamentably saw the "Grim Reaper" carry out his double-barrelled worst, as 219 "ABHAINN NA TOLCHANN" drew to a stand at Cork, with a rake of BREL designed MK3's, forming a special from Heuston. Run in order to cater for additional traffic, generated by returning supporters from the previous day's Cork v Kerry All Ireland football final, which took place at Croke Park. Upon arrival at Kent, the set returned empty to Dublin, the axe prematurely falling against traditional hauled coaching stock. The orange and black vehicles finding their way to rot on rusty sidings within the miserable remains of the yard, which is barely recognisable as North Wall. The 21st also witnessed the first MK 3, Standard 7112 reduced to a pile of scrap in Waterford Yard.

The recent playground of 071s and 201s, with their express trains, along with a supporting cast of 141s and 181s busily marshalling stock; Heuston is now just a graveyard, haunted by ghostly tombstones, in the form of green and silver railcars, which is where our brief story began...

Finally, thanks must be offered to the following people for their help and enthusiasm in compiling this volume.

As the compiling progressed, two fellow photographers became absolutely indispensable 'cogs' within the traction motor of production, for three very important reasons: the sourcing of a selection of amazing colour transparencies, the researching of some of the finer details and, possibly their most significant contribution, the offering of advice on helping make the copy more interesting and succinct. Thus to Colm O'Callaghan and Richard Wall we extend our heartfelt thanks! Peter Jones of the Irish Traction Group (ITG) confirmed one specific point, and last, but *definitely* not least, our thanks to our wives, Ann, Carolyn and Jane, for their continued patience and support while we are out taking pictures. 'France next' – we think they still have loco-hauled trains over there…!

Mark Darby, Neil Higson and Paul Quinlan

If only one could go back to times such as these! In October 1978, passing the most sublime bi-directional semaphore signals, Metropolitan Vickers 'A' No 024 approaches Bog Road level crossing, some 18 miles from Cobh Junction (renamed Glounthaune in November 1994), with beet empties bound for Youghal. Today the 6 miles from Cobh Junction to Midleton are in the process of being reinstated in connection with Cork's rejuvenated suburban system. No 024 lasted until withdrawal at the end of January 1987. *Richard Wall*

On 4 February 1978, with driver Mick Byrne and inspector Brendan Flynn at the helm, No 106 approaches its destination at Bray with the 'Sulzer Requiem' railtour from Dublin Connolly. The tour was run for the Irish Railway Record Society (a most prominent body), whose members enjoyed photographic stops at all stations on the outward trip! The train is passing a fine selection of former Dublin & South Eastern Railway semaphores, which were removed in February 1983 as part of the preparations for Centralised Traffic Control (CTC) resignalling, prior to electrification for the DART scheme. Placed into traffic on 8 November 1956, No 106 became the last class member to receive heavy repairs, entering Inchicore in June 1974 and being out-shopped eight months later in February 1975. Two days after this image was recorded, No 106 found herself diagrammed to the Heuston/North Wall transfer freights when a basic electrical fault prevented the driver from selecting the forward direction. The following day, 7 February, the BRCW locomotive was taken out of service, thus bringing down the final curtain on more than a quarter of a century of Sulzer power in the Republic. *Richard Wall*

What a timeless classic this photograph is! Not all CIÉ branch lines closed in the 1960s, the line to Loughrea being a remarkable survivor until the grim reaper finally took it away from us on 1 November 1975. For much of the diesel era the short branch from Attymon Junction was worked by a Deutz-built 'G' class four-wheeled shunter hauling the 'regular' coach, No 1904, together with one or two wagons as required! From mid-1975 a B201 class locomotive replaced the diminutive German diesels. In this September 1975 view No B220 sits at Loughrea prior to her next trip up to Attymon Junction. No 220 was 'officially' withdrawn on 25 September 1986, scrapping being completed at Vic Berry's, Leicester, during June 1990. *Jonathan Allan*

This photograph illustrates a portfolio of locomotives representing almost the complete history of the first generation of the Republic's main-line diesel fleet, depicting members of the 'A', 'B' and 'C' class. On the bitterly cold morning of 22 October 1993, No 049 passes through Carrick-on-Suir with the 04.45 Mallow to Wellington Bridge beet empties. The photographer notes that the signal box had a number of broken window panes, which would no doubt have contributed to making life uncomfortable for the signalman. The former goods shed in the background has found a new lease of life, now used as the base for the Irish Traction Group. The preserved locomotives on display are unrestored BRCW No B103 and Metropolitan Vickers No C231. The ITG had assumed site responsibility in June of the previous year. *Antony Guppy*

The most important station on the Mallow-Tralee 'Kerry Road', Killarney became a dead-end station in 1859 when the line was extended beyond there to Tralee. Up trains arriving at the station and down trains departing from it have to reverse. They do so using the Check Road, so called because it was once the site of a check platform where trains stopped for passengers' tickets to be checked. On Saturday 3 July 2004, its station work complete at the bay platform behind the photographer on the right, the 12.50 Cork-Tralee has set back into the Check Road. The fantastic sound of an 071 on full power now blankets the whole area, as No 072 charges out of the Check Road and attacks the bank curving away from the station, making for Farranfore. The road is made for the up 14.00 Tralee-Heuston to depart straight from the main platform. These beautiful semaphores were felled under the Tralee line mini-CTC resignalling scheme, commissioned on 25 February 2005. Although the signal cabin with its 36-lever Railway Signal Company frame was abolished as a block post, it is thankfully still extant. Today there are no loco-hauled trains on the Kerry Road. *Paul Quinlan*

Under a late November setting sun in 2004, an unidentified 201 approaches Limerick Junction at the head of a Mark 3 set. By the time IÉ ordered the 201s from GM, the hugely successful 645 series' prime mover was no longer in production. In a competitive marketplace, EMD had needed to offer improved fuel economy, increased power and better reliability than had been delivered by the last-of-line 645F. Its answer was the new 710 engine, so named because of the individual cylinder displacement in cubic inches. A longer piston stroke, redesigned turbocharger and new crankcase were among the improvements on what was, essentially, a reworking and enlargement of the classic 645. In the 12-cylinder variants favoured by IÉ, the 710G3B develops 3,200hp, or 725hp more than the 2,475hp put out by the 645 E3C fitted to the 071. To take advantage of the 201s' 100mph capability, from May 1995 the maximum line speed limit on the Cork road was hoisted from 90 to 100mph. *Paul Quinlan*

No 085 waits for the off at Wellington Bridge on 25 October 1995 with a sugar beet train for Mallow, County Cork. In the background more of the root crop is loaded ready for the next service, a typical view of the era; sadly, on 12 May 2006 the Mallow factory was informed that it was to close with 330 job losses due to the lack of subsidy from the EU. The last train arrived on 1 February that year, so bringing the beet story to a close, having started back in the 1920s when the Irish Government set up factories at Carlow, Mallow, Thurles and Tuam to help kick-start the economy. A viability study was conducted to see if the Mallow factory could make ethanol from sugar beet and wheat, but alas to no avail, as by November 2008 it was being ripped apart, a sad end. *Dave Brush*

No 232 *Abhainn na Chaomaraigh/River Cummeragh* is on the approaches to Killarney near the village of Ballyhar with the 15.15 Tralee to Mallow push-pull service on 21 October 2008. Unusually on this day the loco-hauled and multiple-unit diagrams had been swapped around, thus providing different photographic opportunities for the photographer. The Tralee to Mallow shuttles had been railcars for a number of years, but due to wheel problems on the Class 2700 units a former Dublin area Mark 3 push-pull set was sent in to assist. This arrangement finished in January 2009 as new Class 22000 units became available for the shuttle. The last remaining loco-hauled weekday services on the branch bowed out on 17 January 2009 when the 07.15 Tralee to Heuston and 18.30 return finally went over to the dreaded railcars. *Neil Higson*

No 150, with the customary two coaches, pulls away from Birdhill, County Tipperary, with the 10.30 Ballybrophy to Limerick service on 2 April 1996, having just passed a Roscrea-bound cement train. Birdhill station opened on 23 July 1860 and was not much changed until its closure for goods in September 1963. Today, 149 years on, and trains still stop and serve the small community, holder of the Ireland's Tidiest Village award for 2006-2008! As for No 150, it was scrapped at Inchicore in February 2005, being the second of the 37-strong 141 class to meet the cutter's torch, surprisingly being outlived by the semaphore signals, which still operate today. *Dave Brush*

No 232 *Abhainn na Chaomaraigh/River Cummeragh* stands at Galway with the 11.00 service to Dublin Heuston, minutes before a heavy downpour soaked the photographer. Until the 1990s Galway saw regular flows of Guinness, fertiliser and even fuel to an oil siding in the bus depot. With the 22000 units now being phased in on this route, it has been announced that the station is to be redeveloped in the near future, as part of the Ceannt Station Quarter project. When finished, the rebuilt station will increase from two to three platforms and have 25 bus bays, all enclosed in a 'cathedral'-style design with a full glass roof. Some call it progress! *Mark Davies*

No 191 chatters her way through the attractive gorse cutting at Burnfort (milepost 150), south of Mourne Abbey, on 14 May 1991, hauling an additional train of air-braked cement bogie tanks bound for Cork. Introduced in August 1979, these tanks were the first air-braked stock to operate in Ireland. The letters 'SA' next to the locomotive's number relate to train protection and braking systems installed on the loco: 'S' indicates CAWS, the Continuous Automatic Warning System, which confirms that the loco is permitted to operate under CTC (Centralised Traffic Control) and is equipped with IÉ train radio, while 'A' indicates the fitting of air brakes. This locomotive was scrapped as far back as May 1998 after running away from North Wall, crashing into the Clonsilla head-shunt and catching fire on 17 August 1991. The mysterious circumstances of this incident may never be known, but have kept the rumour mill turning for many years! *Douglas Johnson*

County Maigh Eo remains this photographer's favourite corner of Ireland, partly due to the beautiful scenery, but more importantly to the local railwayman who was responsible for fostering so much interest and enthusiasm in his railway. On the rather wild morning of 17 August 1997, Mayo branch stalwart driver Phelim Lyons makes sure the headlight of No 227 *Abhainn na Leamhna/River Laune* is shining brightly as the 07.30 Sundays-only Westport to Athlone wheels through Cushinsheeaun. This particular Sunday, due to high passenger loadings, the train was booked to run through to Dublin, although the crew only worked the train as far as Athlone, returning with the 10.50 from the Westmeath town. *Mark Darby*

With flowering gorse bushes adding a splash of colour, the empty long-welded-rail discharge train makes its way over the South Wexford line under an ominous sky at Robinstown on Monday 12 May 2003. Powered by No 080, with its trademark rainwater strip above the windscreens, it is returning to Portlaoise having dropped long welded rails on the South Eastern. When finished in the autumn of 2004, this was the last of the radial routes from Dublin to be completely relaid with continuous welded rail (CWR). New rails are imported through Belview Port, where they are loaded onto the 'steel train' to be taken to the rail welding plant at Portlaoise. There they are welded into longer 'strings' for delivery by the discharge train to relaying sites, ultimately being welded in situ to form CWR. Although many of them are now relegated to engineer's trains by the arrival of an incessant stream of new railcars, the 071s have not found favour with the permanent way department; they are difficult to restart with a cold engine, an occupational hazard for locos shut down overnight in far-flung outposts! *Paul Quinlan*

Asahi Limited opened its plant in Killalla, County Mayo, in 1974, with its liner trains to Ballina traditionally the preserve of the Metropolitan Vickers 'A' class, until their untimely demise in April 1995. On the evening of Wednesday 9 July 1997 a pair of 'Small' GMs ('Big' GMs were 'supposedly' too heavy to cross the bridge over the River Moy, at milepost 156), Nos 133 and 148, pass the former ballast pit at Newbridge leading the 19.00 North Wall to Ballina Asahi liner. Acrylonitrile, the highly flammable chemical used in the production of nylon, is being transported in demountable tanks, housed within collision-proof frames and carried on flat wagons fitted with spark-proof brake blocks and wheel guards. The chemical tanks can be seen at the rear of the train. Asahi closed in October 1997, resulting in the loss of a number of freight flows, including coal and oil, which ran up the Western Corridor from Foynes Port. Withdrawal came for No 133 on 27 February 2003; No 148 lasted a while longer, being scrapped in September 2006. *Colm O'Callaghan*

Having spent the day accumulating nearly 300 almost trouble-free miles, to add to the odd million and a half gained prior to retirement, No A39 rests adjacent to the 'military' platform at Heuston terminus. Photographed at around 22.00 on the night of 23 January 1999, A39 had returned to the capital after a jaunt around the South East, with ITG's 'Silver Cloud' railtour. The itinerary included delights such as the viaduct at Thomastown, Waterford's fine signal cabin, and the quayside through Wexford. With more than four decades of sterling service and perambulations covering the whole of the country, the silver 'A' class made history hours earlier, becoming the first Metropolitan Vickers locomotive to negotiate the Lavistown loop, recently opened to negate the necessity for liner trains to reverse at Kilkenny. *Mark Darby*

Showing off its 'fern green' 'InterCity' livery to the full, No 231 *Abhainn na Maighe/River Maigue* thunders past Rocker, just south of Templemore, with the 15.00 Dublin Heuston to Cork service on 30 April 2009. All services on this route are in the hands of these colourful 201s, with a stylish DVT at the Dublin end, and seven Mark 4 coaches sandwiched in between. Built in Beasain, Spain, by CAF in 2004, the DVTs contain two MAN engine/generator sets that provide on-board heating and lighting suitable for rakes of up to 10 vehicles, although they only currently run in sets of eight. At some stage in the future they may be converted into power cars to enable 125mph operations, which the 'River' class locomotives are not capable of attaining. *Neil Higson*

The last scheduled passenger train between Ballina and Limerick ran on 3 April 1976. Twenty-nine years later, the Government finally bowed to a determined public campaign and agreed to reopen the Western Rail Corridor, initially between Athenry and Ennis, with intermediate stations at Craughwell, Ardrahan and Gort. Physical work on the comprehensive rebuilding of the 35¼-mile link commenced from the Athenry end in 2007. It has been a godsend to the surviving Bo-Bos, providing plenty of work on trains of ballast, strings of long welded rail from Portlaoise, and relaying trains. On the morning of 4 July 2008 a relaying train from Gort to that day's work site near Ardrahan is being cautiously propelled towards Kiltartan AHB by Nos 147 and 177, from whose rear cab the train is being driven. A pair of relaying gantries is mounted on the wagon next to the locos. The empty train will later return to Gort for reloading and overnight stabling. In January 2009 it was hoped that railcars would begin passenger services between Limerick and Galway by the summer. As for freight, we shall wait and see. *Paul Quinlan*

This May 1976 image of BRCW No 103 is arguably the most astonishing illustration contained within the pages of this book. The Sulzer is photographed at Kiltimagh (closed to passengers as far back as 17 June 1963) on the erstwhile 'Burma Road' with the weed-spray train returning from Collooney Junction to Claremorris. The 'Burma Road' had closed completely in the first week of November the previous year. As the junction at Collooney had been decommissioned, it was necessary for the BRCW machine to propel the train back as far as Tubbercurry to run round. The photographer, who was fortunate enough to travel in the cab with driver Paddy Neville of Inchicore and guard Liam Cronin, relates several interesting stories of the trip, such as helping the train crew to remove various pieces of fencing blocking the line as farmers attempted to reclaim what they regarded as rightfully theirs, or forcing over the pointwork at Tubbercurry with the aid of crowbars! It is almost certain this was the last train to traverse the section from Collooney Junction to Kiltimagh. Introduced into traffic on 13 August 1956, No 103 was among the final three to be taken out of service, finally bowing out on 17 November 1977. *Richard Wall*

Telegraph poles and a semaphore signal blend beautifully into County Mayo's rural landscape, to remind the viewer of a bygone era. On 25 June 1999 No 219 *Abhainn na Tolchann/River Tolka* passes Cushinsheeaun, a few miles short of journey's end, with the 08.25 Dublin Heuston to Westport service. Unusually the locomotive is only supporting English-language nameplates. Having failed to secure this location in sunshine over three previous years of visits, the sun shone brightly, and my thanks must be extended to the gang of track workers who all obliged and stood shadow-side as the train passed by! *Mark Darby*

No 085, with the standard load of 18 loaded bogie flats, approaches Cherryville Junction with the 07.55 Waterford to Ballina liner service. It will shortly stop at Kildare to run round, then return north-west towards Athlone and Claremorris. The new N7 motorway is visible in the background, which, together with the IÉ policy of only running full container services, has helped devastate intermodal services in Ireland. Within the last 10 years services to Cork, Mallow, Dublin, Limerick, Belfast and many other places have all been lost to road transport. *Mark Davies*

Nos 134 and 153 thunder past Cappagh gates with the 10.50 Limerick-Waterford laden cement train on Saturday 27 September 2003. In accordance with regulations for train marshalling, the two-axle 'bubbles' have been placed at the rear of the four bogie flats; their containers are loaded with infant formula manufactured at the Wyeth facility in Askeaton, and road-hauled from there to Limerick. The cement is destined for the silo at Waterford's Sallypark Yard, but the containers will be tripped the few miles further down to Belview Port for export by sea. Ten days after this shot was taken the Suir Viaduct collapsed, causing these cement wagons to be diverted via Kildare. However, from 29 October they were replaced by Platin-Waterford trains, while Platin-Cork cement began operating from Limerick. The container flow was an inevitable casualty of the new arrangements. No 153 was scrapped in late June 2007. *Paul Quinlan*

On 1 May 2008 No 212 *Abhainn na Slaine/River Slaney*, wearing its revised orange livery, passes Clonyquin on the approach to Portarlington with the 07.15 Galway to Dublin service. The train has just passed over the location where the (3-foot) narrow-gauge peat railways crossed to gain access to the former Portarlington peat-burning power station, the first of its type in Ireland. The Clonsast Co supplied fuel to the ESB power station using mainly Rushton locomotives, the bogs being to the left of the train, the power station to the right. Opened in 1946 by the Bishop of Kildare, its cooling towers dominated the landscape until it was finally demolished on 3 April 1997, after standing derelict for 11 years. *Neil Higson*

A timeless scene, Beauparc on the Drogheda to Navan branch retains much atmosphere of bygone times. On 9 May 1994 No 036, one of seven 'As' uprated to 1,650hp on re-engining, is about to draw forward over the train-crew-operated level crossing with M105, the 10.20 Tara Mines to Dublin Alexandra Road train, containing zinc for export. Tara Mines' rail operation commenced when a short section of the former Navan to Oldcastle branch line was reinstated, from Tara Junction (formerly known as Nevinstown Junction) in June 1977. *Mark Darby*

Even when it's sunny, views of the imposing 1,722-foot-high bulk of Ben Bulben, some 5 miles distant, are often hampered by haze. However, on 6 June 2007 clear light gives rise to this stunning backdrop as No 074 pounds up the MGWR 1862-built short branch from Sligo Quay with the 12.00 WSO Waterford timber train, which is booked a stop en route at Longford to check the straps are tight, just in case the load has settled! Conveying sawn logs for customer Coillte, on arrival at Waterford yard, the timber will be transhipped to Smartply's 350,000m³ plant, where it will be processed into board materials, such as the popular OSB range. Sadly this flow finished on 11 December, with No 082 performing the honours, leaving yet another line with no booked freight. The poet W. B. Yeats, one of Ireland's most famous sons, long associated with Sligo, is buried within the shadow of Ben Bulben. *Mark Few*

During the intervening years since this image was recorded on 13 May 1994, the location to the south of Drogheda station has altered beyond all recognition, as the Drogheda commuter railcar service depot now occupies the area to the right of the tracks. No 036 pulls onto the Belfast to Dublin main line with service M105, the 10.20 Tara Mines to Alexandra Road. These trains, when hauled by an 'A', loaded to 814 tons and conveyed either lead or zinc ore, but never a mixed consist, although both commodities use the same wagons. By January 2009 it was beginning to look as though the Tara Mines branch was set to enter another period of inactivity as the world recession began to bite, the value of the ore being less than the cost of extracting it in the first place! *Mark Darby*

Back in October 1973, when this masterpiece was taken, No 031 was a little over 17 years old and still had a further 18 years of service ahead, being withdrawn in January 1991. The driver checks proceedings as No 031 shunts beet wagons, forming a 'beet pick-up' from Cork to Youghal at Cill laith. The regular daily freight over the branch to Youghal ended in June 1978, with Killeagh ceasing to be a block post just over a year later in October 1979. On the train's return, any loaded wagons above a total of 25 would be left behind at places such as Midleton, as 25 was the maximum permitted load up the bank out of Cork, prior to the train being marshalled at Rathpeacon or Mallow sidings before onward transit to the processing factory. The last beet train to traverse the Youghal branch ran at the end of 1981, hauled by No 049. *Richard Wall*

Wednesday 6 June 2007 sees Nos 149 and 166 ease past the Emly Road Bridge on newly laid concrete sleepers and welded rail, the formation yet to be ballasted! They are hauling the 10.15 Limerick-Waterford laden bulk cement train under the control of driver Ray Collins of Waterford depot, who had earlier worked the 11.50 Waterford-Limerick empty cement up to Limerick Junction; he then collected the laden train, which had been brought down by a Limerick driver.

On 3 June 2008, almost exactly a year after this shot was taken, Nos 149 and 166 were both officially withdrawn. They were cut up at Inchicore two months later, on 19 and 8 August respectively. Fittingly, No 149 donated its power unit to Metrovick No 226, which is being painstakingly restored by the Irish Traction Group in Carrick-on-Suir. *Paul Quinlan*

The Mayo branch boasts some delightful scenery, particularly as it runs adjacent to the shores of Lough Ree, shortly after leaving the Galway line at Athlone West Junction. Captured amid classic County Roscommon scenery, between Knockcroghery and Leacarrow, is No 219 *Abhainn na Tolchann/River Tolka* with a 6+GV set behind her, forming the 13.05 Dublin Heuston to Westport service on 18 August 1997. A few months later, on 8 November, a derailment near this spot highlighted the poor state of the infrastructure along the line. At the time Knockcroghery signal cabin was the fringe box for CTC. Between Monday 16 April and the afternoon of Friday 4 May 2007 the line from Athlone West Junction to Westport and Ballina was closed as modernisation of the branch headed towards completion. The first train to use the newly signalled line was the 16.15 Heuston to Ballina, hauled by No 081 on 4 May. *Mark Darby*

In the summer of 2006 the photographer eagerly looked forward to Friday afternoons, for the opportunity to get a shot of the 13.10 Heuston-Tralee service. At this stage it was always a set of the charismatic Cravens, eking out their final months on workings such as this Fridays-only train and various specials. On 2 June the sight and sound of No 112 justifies his anticipation, as it roars around the curve at Charleville on full power, hauling nine Cravens with a BR van at each end. The loco was then on long-term loan to IÉ. Evidence of attention from Inchicore can be seen in the mismatched cabside windows, radiator fan cowling and LED marker lights. *Paul Quinlan*

Running up the Western Freight Corridor for Asahi Chemicals, the affectionately known 'Coal + Oil' was a popular train. In its latter years less oil was transported, resulting in a coal-only train! On 28 April 1997 the 12.15 Mondays-only Foynes to Ballina service threads gorse-strewn County Galway, near Ballyglunin to the north of Athenry, behind Nos 134 and 123; the empties will return south the following Saturday. Withdrawal of the beloved 'A' class, and double-heading not being permitted on the Foynes branch, saw a second locomotive added upon arrival at Limerick, for the 124-mile run up to County Mayo. During October 1991, with track relaying taking place along the Ballina branch, rail from the Tuam/Claremorris section found itself in North Mayo, which resulted in the line between Ennis and Claremorris closing under extremely controversial circumstances. The resulting closure saw the 'Coal + Oil' diverted via Portarlington. *Colm O'Callaghan*

It's 13 April 1997 and No 167, with its load of railway ballast for engineering work in the area, trundles past a couple of walkers out for a Sunday afternoon stroll. Behind the engine can be seen a 1920s-vintage GS&WR-built plough van, No 8456, which is currently the oldest piece of rolling stock still in operation with Irish Rail, a real scoop for the photographer! The beautiful backdrop is Killiney Bay, which has been compared to the Bay of Naples in Italy. Proving popular with the rich and famous, Van Morrison, The Edge, Bono and Enya are among those who own property in the area. Sadly, on 8 August 1867 a dramatic rail crash known locally as the 'Brandy Hole Accident' occurred on the 'head'. A steam-hauled Enniscorthy to Dublin train ran over a faulty rail joint on the bridge spanning Ram Scalp, causing it to plunge into the sea below! Amazingly only two passengers were killed but 23 were injured.
Antony Guppy

Cork's Kent railway station was built in 1893 for the Great Southern & Western Railway. Originally known as Cork Glanmire Road, it was renamed Kent in 1966 after Thomas Kent, the Irish Nationalist who was executed by the RIC (firing squad) in April 1916 for his part in that year's Easter Rising. In 1979 it was used for filming *The First Great Train Robbery* starring Sean Connery. On 26 July 1995 the then new No 226 *Abhainn an Siuire/River Suir* sits at the head of a train of Mark 3 coaches with a Dublin service. These locomotives have worked these services from new but, as they now operate with push-pull Mark 4s, this picture would only show a DVT nowadays. *Neil Higson*

In common with some other models built in the early to mid-1990s at the London plant for various North American roads, including Santa Fe and Canadian Pacific, the 201s acquired an unenviable reputation for poor build quality. At various times they have been plagued by problems ranging from excessive wheel wear, software glitches in the EM2000 microprocessor control, crankshaft failures, exhaust fires and faulty windscreen wipers, to name only some. Not surprisingly, maintenance staff and drivers do not universally love them! Extensive and expensive overhaul programmes have not achieved significantly improved reliability. A noteworthy modification was carried out on No 233. To reduce exhaust back pressure, its silencer was replaced by a direct to atmosphere exhaust. Impressive results led to plans being developed to modify most of the class, but these had to be abandoned because of warranty issues and concerns about noise, and No 233 was reconverted to standard. The good people of Pallas get an unexpected acoustic treat as it passes, in modified form, with the 13.05 Heuston-Limerick service on Friday 20 May 2005. *Paul Quinlan*

No 082 basks in the sun at Mullingar on Saturday 6 April 2002 with the 13.45 Sligo Quay-North Wall empty Esso liner. The diesel and home heating-oil traffic to Sligo had effectively ceased to operate by the summer of 2005, although latterly it no longer operated as a block train, the wagons running on the Sligo liner. Built in 1920, the signal cabin, with its 65-lever Railway Signal Company frame, was by now one of the largest remaining mechanical cabins on IÉ. The track layout was heavily rationalised in September 2003, in advance of resignalling between Sligo and Maynooth with Mini-CTC in 2005. Under the second and final phase, commissioned on 25 November, the cabin closed. However, it must be manned if any permanent way trains operate over the long-closed former main line to Athlone via Moate, seen in the foreground. While hauling the 17.40 Rosslare-Connolly on 3 October 1979, No 082 ran into the rear of an empty bagged cement train that was shunting in Arklow. Although it suffered serious cab damage, Inchicore got it back into traffic by 22 December!
Paul Quinlan

Galway and Westport services were transferred by CIÉ to the Portarlington route out of Heuston as far back as 1973. Before that, trains for Galway and Mayo commenced their journey from Pearse, which subsequently became downgraded to a commuter station. The upgrading of the Portarlington to Athlone route in the 1980s, together with the closure of Athlone Midland station in 1985, brought passengers back to the former GS&WR station, on the opposite side of the River Shannon, for the first time since 1927. The former MGWR main line from Mullingar sadly became little more than a through siding, although 'mails' from Connolly briefly continued to ply the erstwhile Midland artery. Traversing the currently mothballed route in this 18 December 1982 image, No 047, complete with tablet-catcher, presents a beautiful sight, picking her way through snowy conditions as she passes the impressive former Midland goods store at Moate. The 'A' is working the 04.30 Ballina to North Wall Asahi liner, which was the final scheduled working over the line. The consist of the liner is most interesting, conveying containers, acrylonitrile tanks, empty coal containers and two demountable oil tanks attached at the rear. From Monday 2 November 1987, the Asahi was re-routed via Portarlington.

Rather interestingly, the final passenger trains to call at Moate were the up and down Galway night mails, which crossed at midnight. Lamentably, these services ceased to serve the Westmeath town in the spring of 1987, after which they too were sent via Portarlington. The final rites were on 16 May, although during the final week of operation no passenger accommodation was included in the train consist. It is a great shame that Moate is not part of the Transport 21 scheme. *Aidan McDonnell*

Opposite: In the photographer's own words, Saturday 27 June 1992 was a busy day at Arklow. During the early 1990s trains were booked to cross at Enniscorthy; however, due to a series of events this busy scene was duly recorded at the County Wicklow town. No 021, working the 13.35 Dublin Connolly to Rosslare service, was running 90 minutes down due to her engine overheating. This resulted in No 012, which had charge of the 17.00 zinc empties to Tara Mines, being substituted for the rest of the trip to County Wexford. No 012 is crossing with the 14.55 Rosslare to Dublin Connolly service, recently arrived behind No 152. In the siding No 021 recuperates with a rake of empty zinc wagons. Due to high charges at the Port of Dublin, zinc traffic had just begun trialling from Tara Mines to the port at Arklow, transported in 20-foot-long demountable red containers covered by blue tarpaulins. The train departed Navan in the early afternoon, travelling as far as Pearse, to stable overnight, with departure from the Dublin commuter station booked for 05.30 the following morning. Owing to lengthy turn-round times at the unloading point, the service only lasted for six weeks. After arriving with the zinc, the locomotive ran light to Shelton Abbey to work the 09.40 empty ammonia tanks to Marino Point. At the time Arklow boasted a fine example of a former DW&WR signal cabin, which housed a 16-lever McKenzie & Holland frame, with access provided directly from the footbridge! In April 2008 the cabin closed, and the semaphores were swept away as the tentacles of CTC spread. *Colm O'Callaghan*

Left: On 7 May 1995 No 147 is employed on the 10.10 Cork to Cobh service as it passes the huge Irish Fertiliser Industries (IFI) chemical plant at Marino Point near Cork. This facility produced the ammonia that was transported in the famed LPG trains of the 1980s and early '90s. Sadly 1995 was the last year for loco haulage of the passenger trains on the 11-mile run between Cork and Cobh, as the 1993 Class 2600 units, built by the Tokyo Car Corporation of Japan, had arrived in the area to take over; in later years these were themselves ousted by the Class 2700 units. *Antony Guppy*

Claremorris is the setting for No 154 as it arrives with the 14.11 empty coaching stock from Manulla Junction on 24 March 1997. To many, Claremorris typified the Irish Railway system with its low-key friendly atmosphere, plenty of activity and semaphore signals in every direction. It was once a major junction for Westport and Ballina to the west, Athlone and Dublin east, Athenry and Limerick south and Collooney to the north. Sadly, as freight traffic dwindled, the south and north lines fell into disrepair, which resulted in a run-down feel to the place. Fortunately, with the Western Corridor scheme these lines will hopefully reopen for both passenger and freight, bringing Claremorris into the 21st century, even if the projected completion date is not until 2014 – but don't expect to see any Class 141s or semaphores! *Dave Brush*

Running 10 minutes ahead of time, No 182 blasts noisily away from Birdhill on Monday 28 May 2001 at the head of the 12.40 Kilmastulla-Mungret Cement Factory Siding laden shale. Three sets are used, normally of eight wagons, for the three return trips that operate Monday to Friday, so that when a train arrives at either end of the trip another set is waiting for the loco to haul away on the return journey. At Kilmastulla the shale is tipped directly into the open wagons from quarry dump trucks, which draw up at a high loading bank above the train. On arrival at the Irish Cement factory in Mungret, the wagons are hooked off so each one can be individually unloaded on the tippler. At the time of writing (March 2009) this traffic is one of only five remaining freight flows on IÉ. No 182 did not live to see this sad state of affairs; in July 2006 it was stripped for spares at Inchicore, and was cut up on the 21st of the following month. *Paul Quinlan*

An unidentified 'A' runs along the Lough Mahon causeway near Marino Point chemical plant, Cobh, minutes after starting its long journey to Shelton Abbey with the ammonia tanks on the delightful evening of 23 April 1990. Sadly, weak ammonia prices coupled with high gas costs in 2002 meant that the facility, together with Shelton Abbey, became unviable, pushing IFI into liquidation. The last train ran on 16 October 2002, hauled by 'Enterprise'-livered 'River' class No 207 with five wagons and the standard barrier at each end. Departing at 10.02 on that sad day, it brought a sunset on locomotive use on the Cork to Cobh section, as by that date all passenger services had gone over to unit operation. *Douglas Johnson*

Introduced into traffic barely a month previously, No 213 sits just proud of the train shed at Corcaigh prior to taking A221, the 17.30 express, up to Dublin Heuston on 26 November 1994. Clearly visible through the cab window is the green LED read-out, which forms part of the display of the locomotive's EM2000 digital traction computer. No 213 had yet to receive her *Abhainn na Muaidhe/River Moy* nameplates. It seems ludicrous that a mere 15 years after their introduction the non-push-pull-fitted examples such as this machine are looking at a life of premature retirement. *Mark Darby*

A few miles north of the town of Mullingar lays Lough Owel, which, at approximately 4 miles long and 2 miles wide, is popular with fishermen for its fine stock of brown trout. With her headlight glowing brightly in the dwindling light, No 076 skirts the shoreline with the 18.15 Sligo to Dublin Connolly service, as the last rays of the day's sunshine cast long shadows on 25 May 1996. Allowing for the time, which was approaching almost 20.15, together with the limitations of a medium-format camera using relatively slow film, this is a very well executed photograph. *Antony Guppy*

No 202 *Abhainn na Laoi/River Lee* runs past the small hamlet of Cushinkeel a few miles east of Westport, powering the 08.20 Dublin Heuston to Westport service on 4 June 2007. No 202 is wearing the revised full-yellow-end version of the original orange and black livery now worn by all ten machines that are non-push-pull-fitted and likely to be dedicated to freight operation in the near future. Dominating the horizon is Nephin, popular with walkers; standing at 806 metres (2,646 feet), it is the second highest mountain in the Nephin Beg mountain range overlooking County Mayo. *Mark Few*

With a rake of matching Mark 2ds, which had been in service since 1972, No 003 approaches the former Liffey Junction with the first train of the day from Sligo, the 07.30 to Dublin Connolly, on 30 September 1988. The site where the main line to the former Midland Great Western Railway terminus at Broadstone diverged lies just behind the photographer, with the train taking the alignment that used to be the branch. Sligo services had succumbed to Rotem Inter City 22000 class railcars, built in Korea, by early December 2007. The semaphore signals behind the train were rendered redundant on 17 February 1991, with the implementation of CTC between Liffey Junction and Clonsilla. *Colm O'Callaghan*

For three-quarters of the year, Wellington Bridge in County Wexford enjoyed life as a quiet, sleepy railway backwater; however, the onset of early autumn brought about a mad increase in the traffic running around the narrow lanes and roads leading to the station as they became jammed with lorries and tractors hauling trailers full of local gold – sugar beet! On the cold but sunny afternoon of 22 October 1993, No 049 positions a rake of travel-weary, Bulleid-designed, upturned four-wheeled wagons beneath the specialised loading apparatus. As soon as the locally produced beet was fully loaded, the trains were off to the processing plant at Mallow, well over 100 miles to the west. *Antony Guppy*

NIR-owned No 209 *River Foyle*, in 'Enterprise' livery, has just crossed the viaduct over the River Nore as it powers away from Thomastown with the late-running 07.30 Heuston-Waterford service on 2 November 2001. The early Mark 2 stock had been obtained from Vic Berry's Leicester scrapyard in 1990, in exchange for redundant 201-class locos. Extensively refurbished at Inchicore, they were a stopgap measure to help ease a severe shortage of rolling stock. They would last until late 2003, when new CAF railcars saw them off. Behind the loco is a former 'Dutch' van, converted to an Electric Generator Van and air-braked to run with the ex-BR stock. *Paul Quinlan*

Photographed from the remains of an unidentified medieval burial mound on 28 June 1993, 'A' class No 036 makes slow progress through the County of Meath, at Nobber, with M191, the 10.45 Kingscourt to Platin train, comprising 15 vacuum-braked hoppers loaded with gypsum. The Kingscourt branch boasted 12 train-crew-operated crossing gates and a maximum speed of 20mph. The schedule was punishing for the locomotive, as a heavy strain was placed on the main generator. During the strike action by ILDA, the Irish Locomotive Drivers Association, much of the traffic was lost to road haulage, and the final scheduled gypsum train to traverse the line ran on 30 October 2001. *Douglas Johnson*

A few miles downstream from Waterford, the unmistakable sound of an 071 rolls across the tranquil waters of the River Suir as No 072 brings a rake of empty beet wagons back to Wellington Bridge. The wagons themselves have an interesting story to tell that speaks volumes for the very positive attitude the railway once had towards freight, at a time when money was very scarce. By the mid-1980s the loose-coupled open wagons used on beet trains were reaching the end of their lives, and unbraked trains were being phased out. To replace them, Limerick Wagon Works turned out 165 new wagons by ingeniously reusing the steel bodywork from two of the old opens, welding one above the other, placing them on a redundant vacuum-braked 'conflat', and adding some bracing! The resulting 'new' wagons consigned loose-coupled beet trains to history, and were a huge success when introduced with the 1985 campaign. Alas, it seems the more investment money that flowed into the railway, the less interest it had in handling freight. The collapse of the Irish sugar industry made these distinctive wagons redundant and, with no alternative use, they were scrapped at the end of 2006 in Mallow and Wellington Bridge. *Paul Quinlan*

The signalman closes the crossing gates to make the road for the 09.35 Limerick-Waterford, ready to depart from Tipperary on 24 August 2000. The photographer waits anxiously, mere feet away from an angry Alsatian with a dislike of enthusiasts! It was not a vantage point that would be chosen again! No 150 had been named during an open day at Inchicore in June 1996 to mark the 150th anniversary of the works. Two *Inchicore Works 150 1846-1996* nameplates and two reading *Ardlanna Inse Chaoír 150 1849-1996* were fitted to alternate cabsides, and the locomotive carried the plates for about two years, the only 'Small' GM to do so. No 150 met its fate at the hands of the scrap-man in February 2005. *Paul Quinlan*

On 6 October 1995, after a night of high winds and torrential rain that saw suspension of ferry sailings between Fishguard and Rosslare, daybreak ushered in some respite. Sporting evidence of a minor front-end skirmish, No 142 sits at a rain-lashed Rosslare Harbour with the stock forming that day's A461, the 07.15 service to Waterford, by rail a distance slightly shy of 40 miles. During the summer timetable at that time this service was booked to continue through to Tralee.

The 'new' station at Rosslare Harbour was completed in 1989, when Rosslare Harbour Mainland closed; it subsequently became 'Europort' in 1996. The honour of the final train to depart from Europort, adjacent to the Harbour terminal buildings, fell to the railcar-formed 07.40 to Dublin on 14 April 2008. By the end of the month, and with the introduction of CTC, a faceless 'platform' some distance from the original terminus had been brought into use. *Mark Darby*

The station at Manulla Junction closed in 1963, but reopened in November 1988. Having no public access, it serves only as a transfer point for passengers between the Ballina branch and the main line to Westport. Because there was no loop here, the branch train from Ballina continued empty to Claremorris to run round, returning empty to Manulla to form the branch connection back to Ballina. Having worked into this lonely outpost with the 13.00 service from Ballina on Thursday 10 August 2006, No 081 is waiting for the 13.05 Westport-Heuston service to clear the section to Claremorris. No 081 entered Diesel One at Inchicore in October 2006 for a major overhaul, re-entering service on 24 April 2007 as the first loco to wear the new black and silver livery. On 9 December 2006 the 13.00 service from Ballina was the last run for the Cravens on the branch set, worked by driver Dessie Gallagher and guard Noel Enright, to be replaced by a railcar. The layout at Manulla Junction was altered and the signal cabin on the platform abolished under the Mayo line Mini-CTC resignalling project, commissioned on 4 May 2007. *Paul Quinlan*

No 220 *An Abhainn Dhubh/River Blackwater* rattles the windows of a small cottage at Oghill near Monasterevan on 2 May 2008, having just left the main lines at Cherryville Junction with the 15.05 Dublin Heuston to Waterford service. No 220 was the last loco to wear the original 1994 orange and black livery at the time but, being push-pull-fitted, it now wears the green 'InterCity' colours. On its approach to Waterford it will run next to the River Blackwater, its English namesake, but oddly its Irish name, An Abhainn Dhubh, is a river on the island of Lewis in the Outer Hebrides! *Neil Higson*

Foynes, a deep-water port on the south bank of the Shannon Estuary, has over the years witnessed flows of many diverse commodities. It is also steeped in much modern-day history. On 9 March 1999 'Small' GM No 189 sits at the head of a rake of wagons that are being loaded with bagged fertiliser from local firm Gouldings of Askeaton. Once loaded, the train will proceed to Limerick Check and on to Athenry, its eventual destination via the Western Corridor. During the heady days of transatlantic air travel, flying boats made Foynes their final call before continuing on to America, and bearing testimony to this the terminal is now a museum in their honour. Coffee containing a touch of whiskey comforted cold and weary travellers of the time, and thus the world-renowned 'Irish coffee' was born! The railway reached Foynes in April 1858, and the station closed for business on 4 February 1963. Although still 'officially' part of the rail network, the branch is now mothballed, the turnout being removed at Limerick Check on 3 November 2007. As for the locomotive, the history books will confirm that No 189 was laid to rest in May 2008. *Colm O'Callaghan*

No 213 *Abhainn na Muaidhe/River Moy*, the first of the class to feature a full yellow end in February 2005, hammers through Ballinillaun with the 11.00 Galway to Dublin Heuston service on 26 October 2006, hauling the former International Mark 3A 'Cu Na Mara' set. With export in mind, ten coaches were built in 1987 by BREL at Derby Litchurch Lane as a development of the standard Mark 3. Initially used on a Euston-Manchester diagram, the 'International Set' soon fell out of favour and was put to use as test coaches during the Class 89 project. Eventually falling into disuse, they were sold in 1994 to Irish Railways. Regauging to 5ft 3in and refurbishment followed at Inchicore, but the planned DVT conversion never materialised, so train supply was supplied by a standard Mark 3 generator van. The remaining nine 'Cu Na Mara' vehicles spent most of their career on the Galway route, but by 2008 they had been stood down and put into store at Dublin North Wall with an uncertain future. *Mark Davies*

Escaping train heat steam, together with low hanging mist and fog, combine forces to create a rather damp and dismal ambience! No 036 emerges from beneath Kilkenny's fine train shed as she runs around the Cravens coaching stock forming B222, the 08.00 Bray to Cork and Dublin train, the Irish Traction Group's 'Beet Campaigner' railtour, which ran via Waterford and Limerick Junction on 26 November 1994. The headboard sported by the Metropolitan Vickers locomotive throughout the seasonal trip over some traditional 'beet lines' depicted a classic portrayal of an 'A', and had been hand-painted by Mark Alden. The interest in the motive power is obvious, given the amount of photographers recording No 036's movements. *Mark Darby*

The foothills of the Galtee Mountains providing a backdrop, on 2 September 2000 the 09.35 Limerick-Waterford service runs off the Suir Viaduct into Cahir, led by No 166. A laden beet train ran away through Cahir in December 1955, demolished a buffer block, and crashed through the viaduct floor into the Suir, tragically killing driver Cornelius Kelly and fireman Francis Frahill of Limerick depot. Three years after this photo was taken, in October 2003, a Waterford-bound cement train would derail on the bridge, 12 wagons falling through the deck onto the riverbank, thankfully without injury. No 166 would be scrapped in August 2008. *Paul Quinlan*

Arguably the most bizarre retirement venue in the world for any locomotive fell to No 055. With more than 37 years' service, and having covered approximately one and a half million miles countrywide, No A55's final resting place became the relaxed surroundings of a town bar! Hell's Kitchen is a public house in Castlerea, which doubles as a railway museum. At the helm is owner Sean Browne, the most genial host, whose vision and perseverance brought about this most amazing phenomenon. On Tuesday 7 July 1998, preceded by the local brass and reed band, No 055 *Sarah* (all the 'As' unofficially received girls' names) arrived on the back of a low-loader from Dublin, to be met by hundreds of bemused onlookers, while several national Irish daily newspapers reported on the Metrovick's arrival.

Sarah was purchased for her scrap value of 1,623 IR£, a small proportion of the project's total cost of 130,000 IR£, 35,000 IR£ of which came from the Roscommon county enterprise board. Placing an 82-ton locomotive partially within the confines of an existing building was no mean feat, but presented the architect, Udo Humborg, with few problems. No A55 has now spent more than 10 years as the centre of attraction at Castlerea, and a visit is strongly advised, not only for the unique opportunity of a Metrovick for company, but also the landlord's hospitality and railway-related conversation, which is world class! On 16 August 1993, during her incarnation as a working locomotive, No 055 blasts through Malahide with M105, the 10.20 Tara Mines to Alexandra Road train. *Antony Guppy*

The steeply graded 1¼-mile-long branch to Silvermines left the Killonan Junction to Ballybrophy line at Silvermines Junction between Birdhill and Nenagh. It was opened in 1966 by CIÉ to transport zinc ore for Canadian company Mogul to the port of Foynes, but sadly this traffic ceased when the firm suffered the ignominy of liquidation in 1982. Barytes was also extracted from Silvermines, being similarly transported by rail to Foynes. Barytes (or barite) is a mineral that is predominantly used within the gas and oil drilling industry as a lubricant and to a lesser extent as a constituent of the barium meal medical application! This view, dating from 18 July 1990, depicts No 039 arriving at Silvermines with the 13.30 empties from Foynes. Due to the restricted length of the siding at Foynes it was necessary to split the train into three portions for unloading. The unique wagons used for the flow enabled a mechanical shovel to literally 'shove' the load out! The final train of barytes ran on 1 November 1993. *Colm O'Callaghan*

The low winter sun casts long shadows from the remains of Dunbrody Abbey, the Cistercian monastery founded in 1170 after the Norman invasion of Ireland. The railway intruded into this peaceful scene when the Fishguard & Rosslare Railways & Harbours Company opened its line from Rosslare Strand to Abbey Junction, Waterford, in 1906. A favourite location of the photographer during the beet campaign, a laden beet train could be heard long before it finally came into view, as the loco worked hard over the grades on the South Wexford. On 14 December 2001 No 080 disturbs the cold still air as it drops down to the bridge over the Campile River. *Paul Quinlan*

Covered in oil, typical of the era, No 026 leaves Wicklow with K202, the Shelton Abbey to Marino Point ammonia empties, on 1 April 1993. The train is crossing Broad Lough on a five-span lattice girder bridge, which was replaced by a rather austere concrete structure between Friday 23 and Sunday 25 July 1993, the Dublin to Rosslare line losing a bit more character in the process.

Into traffic as silver No A26 in March 1956, its Crossley engine would be its prime mover until November 1971. The last 'A' to be re-engineered with a new GM 12-645E engine, No A26r would soldier on until August 1994 when it was finally stopped, scrapping being completed by July 1995 when a mere 38 years old! *Douglas Johnson*

A view seldom appreciated by mortals, other than drivers, is that from the footplate. Prior to enjoying the 92 miles to Maynooth in the cab of NIR's No 112 *Northern Counties*, this photograph was obtained of No 086 arriving at Boyle with A902, the 13.35 Dublin Connolly to Sligo service, on 15 July 1995. The Northern Irish interloper found itself in County Roscommon leading the ITG-operated 'Early Bird' railtour, which had arrived in Mullingar by way of the former Midland & Great Western line from Athlone behind a pair of 'Small' GMs, Nos 131 and 124. These had powered the train from Bray, with No 112 subsequently working forward to Sligo, before hauling the return working back to Bray. *Mark Darby*

Approaching the important junction station of Portarlington, known to generations of railwaymen as 'Port', No 088 makes an impressive sight as it coasts over the River Barrow with the 18-bogie Norfolk liner from Ballina to Waterford. The waterway forms the border between the counties of Offaly and Laois at this point. By 7 December 2007 the 'Norfolks' were like the elusive pot of gold at the end of the rainbow – much sought after by enthusiasts, as by now they were the sole container trains operating in Ireland. The final member of the 071 class, No 088 would be repainted into black and silver at Inchicore in September 2008. *Paul Quinlan*

No 206 *Abhainn na Life/River Liffey*, one of six class 201s dedicated for use between Dublin and Belfast on the 'Enterprise' passenger services, pulls away from Athenry with the 09.10 Dublin to Galway service on 26 October 2006. These locos often strayed from their dedicated border diagrams due to engine wear brought on by having to maintain the head-end power for train heating, resulting in the engines working harder for long periods, Control's answer to this being to spread such use across the 201 fleet. With the mandatory use of TPWS north of the border, this has now been curtailed as only 'Enterprise' 201s are fitted with this equipment. Athenry is now back on the rail map as an important junction town with the opening of the Western Corridor link from Limerick, and with the possible reopening north to Claremorris more trains will pass through. Hopefully the cement terminal, closed in 2001, may also see reactivation! *Neil Higson*

Amid the desolation, Metropolitan Vickers No 210 runs round its weed-spray train at Newcastle West, on the North Kerry line, on the evening of Thursday 8 June 1978. The train had previously arrived in Limerick at midday, having run from Athenry. It then sprayed the Foynes branch and stabled overnight. The following morning the train proceeded via Barnagh (now part of a scenic heritage trail) to Tralee and Fenit. After a very intensive programme, Mallow was reached later that evening. The common practice of the loco supporting detachable high-visibility warning boards began with this train. With the exception of the former station house, this scene has totally disappeared beneath a housing estate. Newcastle West closed to passengers in February 1963, with the Ballingrane Junction to Listowel section closing to all traffic on 3 November 1975. The remaining North Kerry line closed in stages between November 1975 and June 1978. No 210 succumbed to the accountant's pen at the end of November 1983. *Richard Wall*

Having run round her train of loaded sugar beet next to the main platform at Limerick Junction, No 150 resumes the journey to the processing plant at Mallow, heading away from the South signal cabin on the afternoon of 22 October 1993. The train started out from Waterford at 12.30. Judging by the external appearance of the 'Small' GM, a recent release from attention at Inchicore had taken place! The scene that greets the present-day photographer at 'the Junction', or 'The Black Hole' as it is frequently referred to, is far more stark, as the entire South Yard, where the cement 'blues' are stabled, has been lifted as part of the resignalling plan. At the time of writing (spring 2009)

Limerick Junction remained a semaphore-signalled oasis on the otherwise CTC-controlled Dublin to Cork main line, the 'Black Hole' reference relating to the fact that trains literally disappear from the controller's screen as they pass through! CTC was intended to finally swallow up the Junction before 2009 was out. The coaches in the siding to the right of the train are timber-bodied, and awaiting their final trip to Inchicore for a date with the scrap-man, their final diagrams having been between Limerick and Rosslare. Timber-bodied stock fell into disfavour as a result of the accidents at Buttevant and Cherryville. *Antony Guppy*

Navan ('An Uaimh') lies at the confluence of the Rivers Boyne and Blackwater. To span the former, the GNR(I) built a 406-foot-long viaduct, completed in 1849 and constructed by Moore Brothers to a design by Sir John MacNeill. On the morning of 7 June 2007 No 074 accelerates over the structure at the head of M105, the 10.20 Tara Mines to Alexandra Road train. The previous day the same locomotive was observed at Sligo on a timber train bound for Waterford! Due to the fluctuating world price of zinc, the trains run accordingly, ceasing completely in November 2001 and not returning until 24 September 2002. *Mark Few*

To cater for weekend travellers, the 17.05 Heuston-Limerick service was extended to Ennis on Fridays. Because some 071s had caused long delays while their weak compressors built up air pressure on the Mark 3 sets, Limerick shed preferred to put on a double for the run to Ennis. The 50-mile return trips were to be the last scheduled passenger turns for the American Bo-Bos, the 17.05 finally going over to railcars in December 2008. The beautiful summer evening of 16 June 2006 sees Nos 149 and 160 working hard up the short bank past Granaghanbeg Lough, near the long-closed Ballycar station, with the Fridays-only 19.25 Limerick-Ennis service. This location is notoriously prone to flooding, causing the railway to close for seven weeks in early 2008. The two locos were cut up at Inchicore within weeks of one another in August 2008. *Paul Quinlan*

There cannot be many sights and sounds more stirring than an 'A' hard at work. Pioneer 'A' No 001, introduced into service on 27 September 1955, powers around Bray Head with service A602, the 13.35 Dublin Connolly to Rosslare Harbour. The cosmopolitan town of Bray forms a pleasing backdrop on a clear 16 May 1992. The later Mark 2ds that formed the working had already witnessed some 20 years of service, eventually bowing out in the Republic in March 2008. The final diagrams for the coaches were selected Dublin to Galway and Athlone trips. *Douglas Johnson*

At Limerick Junction on Tuesday 29 August 2000 the driver of No 155 slows the 09.35 from Limerick on the approach to Keane's Points, where it will diverge to serve the station. Once its work there is complete, the train will reverse out to here, before resuming the journey eastwards to its destination at Waterford. Keane's Points were named after Richard Keane, a pointsman employed here in the early years of the Waterford & Limerick Railway. The track on the right is a loop, the double line from here to Killonan Junction near Limerick having been singled as an economy measure in 1929. In the distance can be seen the crossing-keeper's hut at Milltown Crossing, where the direct curve from the Dublin-Cork line comes in from the right. It opened in October 1967 and is now controlled from CTC in Connolly. No 155 was stripped for spares at Inchicore in October 2006, and was cut up at the end of the following month. *Paul Quinlan*

No 204 *Abhainn na Coiribe/River Corrib* has no difficulty keeping the 12.00 Dublin North Wall-Cork North Esk liner rolling quietly past Holycross on Friday 25 June 2004. As an omen of things to come, there is not a container in sight – within 13 months no further containers would move by rail south of Portarlington. The four vacuum-braked bogie wagons are carrying kegs of draught beer from the world-famous Guinness brewery at St James's Gate. The decision of major customer Diageo, the Guinness parent company, not to renew its contract was another nail in the coffin for rail freight, and the movement of beer by rail ceased at the end of August 2006. *Paul Quinlan*

The delightful combination of Nos 143 and 121 growls up the bank at Taylorstown, County Wexford, with the 12.15 'Beet' from Wellington Bridge to Mallow on 28 October 1995. The wagons are in a typical state of loading, full until the contents start to fall out, but who would have thought that within 11 years both the engines and wagons would have been reduced to scrap!

The photographers had arrived a little late to take this picture, so a mad dash across three fields ensued, noticing the farmer running away and hiding under a hedge in the process! He later approached them to ask what they were up to, initially believing they were criminals involved in something dubious on his land, as he had not realised what the tripods were! *Dave Brush*

Like a lot of places, Nenagh used to receive cement by rail on an 'as required' basis. Sadly, bagged cement was lost (or thrown away) by rail in September 2004, so sights like this are gone for ever. No 190 is seen easing back towards the unloading bay with the 08.45 from Castlemungret Cement Works, Limerick, on 2 April 1996. After unloading half the cement, the train will then set off 20 miles up the line to Roscrea to deliver the rest! The delightful little 20-tonne four-wheel Irish Cement pallet vans totalled more than 150, but by the looks of the angle of the back wagon the fleet size was about to drop by one! *Dave Brush*

Left: A site that requires official paperwork to indulge in photography is the Tara Mines export terminal at Alexandra Road, within the docks complex at Dublin. With the necessary permit in the photographer's back pocket, this portrait of No 026 was duly secured on 9 May 1994. The 'A' has run round M107, the 13.20 from Tara Mines, and has commenced propelling the stock containing ore towards the unloading traverser. Known as slip working, the empty uncoupled wagons set back individually by means of gravity onto a separate road, where they are then recoupled and formed into the return working, going forward for either reloading back at the mine, or stabling at Drogheda. *Mark Darby*

Opposite: No 085 climbs through the fittings at Cherryville Junction with the 18-wagon 07.55 Waterford to Ballina 'Norfolk' on Thursday 1 May 2008. This 221-mile service, now the last container flow in Ireland, runs three times a week on behalf of the shipping company Norfolk Line, which has a base at Waterford Belview, now the busiest container terminal outside Dublin. This has enabled it to keep running trains when sadly all other ports have fallen to using road for their transportation needs, but the building of the dedicated road link to the N25 Euroroute will no doubt have a negative effect on rail. *Neil Higson*

Until recent years a very sparse passenger service operated over the secondary line from Limerick Junction to Waterford. The poor offering was doubled in the summer months by the addition of one return morning train! This opened up the chance to capture a picture at Bohercrow where, on a fine clear day, the Galtee Mountains – Ireland's highest inland mountain range – provide a scenic backdrop. Galteemore, at 3,009 feet the highest peak in the range, rises above the last carriage of the train, made up of the usual BR van and two Cravens. No 145 is nearing the summit of the brief climb towards Limerick Junction, just over 2 miles away, with the Summer-only 07.05 Rosslare-Limerick service on Tuesday 28 August 2001. Services on this line are now more frequent, being exclusively railcar-operated since September 2004. No 145 submitted to the cutter's torch in August 2006. *Paul Quinlan*

Bell liner container traffic was probably the best known of the liner trains in the Republic. On Saturday 2 April 1994 No 158 powers away from Cherryville Junction with the 13.00 North Wall to Waterford Bell liner. During 28 October 1996 extremely high winds battered the south-east, blowing one of the overhead gantry cranes at Belview Port onto a second, which ultimately collapsed and blocked the line to Rosslare Strand! The Waterford to Rosslare line remained closed until 11 November. Bell liners ceased running when the company went into liquidation in July 1997. No 158 lasted a little longer, being scrapped in March 2003. *Colm O'Callaghan*

Beneath a wonderfully alluring sky, a 141/181 'combo' heads away from the capital's conurbation on 29 April 2008. Nos 146 and 190 are photographed plodding over the River Barrow at Monasterevan while working a ballast train bound for the Western Corridor rebuilding project.

Immediately behind the photographer's vantage point at this well-known location on the Dublin to Cork main line an aqueduct conveys the Grand Canal, Athy branch, over the river. Waterborne traffic using the man-made waterway made Monasterevin a most prosperous place. *Antony Guppy*

If any event could lay claim to sowing the seeds of my love of the Republic's railways, the honour has to be shouldered by the man leaning out of the cab of No 223 *Abhainn na hAinnire/River Anner* at Westport – Phelim Lyons, a Westport-based driver of 40 years' service who retired in 2001. A chance conversation with him as he was preparing to drive the up Dublin express away from the Mayo town one morning in the mid-1990s left me with an amazing feeling of how an employee with so many years under his belt could still advocate and be full of so much enthusiasm for 'his' railway. Further visits over subsequent years followed, and Phelim always had as much time as was necessary to enthuse about all things 'Mayo branch'. On Sunday 17 August 1997 Phelim reverses No 223 out of Westport, in a scene that had stood beautifully still for more than 30 years (motive power excepted, of course!) The 201 had arrived earlier at the head of the 10.50 Sundays-only service from Athlone. Coupled next to the locomotive is one of the Werkspoor-designed 'Dutch' heating vans, which are colloquially known as 'Sherman Tanks'! *Mark Darby*

The staff for the section from Clonmel has just been deposited at the red-bricked shed beside the signalman, who holds up the staff for the section to Limerick Junction, as Nos 124 and 167 roll through Tipperary on 8 October 2004 with the 10.10 Wellington Bridge-Mallow laden beet train, almost spot on time. It was important to stay in path because the 54¾-mile single line from Waterford to Limerick Junction had only three intermediate crossing loops. To enable the improved service of three passenger trains each way to negotiate this congested stretch, long waits could be experienced by the beet trains – normally five laden on Monday to Saturday plus their return empties during the 2004 beet campaign. The 10.10 lay in Waterford for more than 90 minutes to await the arrival of the 10.40 passenger from Limerick Junction, then sat for nearly 50 minutes in Clonmel to cross the 12.40 Limerick-Waterford passenger. Although its mechanical interlocking was extensively refurbished in 2002, Tipperary is due to become redundant as a block post in 2009 under the Limerick Junction resignalling scheme. At the time of writing (February 2009), No 167 is happily still with us on Heuston pilot duties. *Paul Quinlan*

Rail/rail crossings on the level have always been very much of an anachronism. The driver of No 172, which has picked up a 'wonky' buffer, receives the staff from the signalman for the section covering Limerick North to Tipperary. The train, the Cravens-composed 15.25 Limerick to Rosslare on Saturday 14 September 2002, will then proceed directly across the Dublin to Cork main line, in the immediate foreground. Four years later, the result of a contretemps within Kilmastulla Shale sidings, cab and frame damage saw a premature end to the Bo-Bo's employment. Following removal of useful parts, including traction motors, No 172's 45-year career came to an end in late January 2007. Unfortunately the coaches have also faded into history. The semaphore signals visible behind the train, situated at Keane's Points, are set to become part of railway folklore as 'the Junction' was set to become fully integrated into CTC before 2009 was out! *Paul Quinlan*

Utilising short-wheelbase tank wagons, which look perfectly suited to a Hornby train set, the 'Sligo Oil' was a photographer's dream – it was, however, an operator's nightmare! Restricted to 35mph running throughout, the train presented pathing problems. On 9 May 1994, with less than 12 months of service remaining, No 012 departs from the yard at North Wall, Dublin, with L904, the 15.20 loaded tanks bound for the Esso terminal at Sligo Quay. The 135-mile journey to the north-west ran on Mondays and Wednesdays, with the same locomotive booked to work the empties back the following day. As a block train, the oils to Sligo ceased on 3 June 2003, although tanks continued to be attached to the Sligo liner for a while longer. Eighteen of the dedicated tanks succumbed in September 2005, the remainder in January 2006. On the left an oil-stained No 026 waits for the 'all clear' to proceed with M107 into the docks complex, bound for Alexandra Road. Together with No 003, No 012 lasted until the final day of Metropolitan Vickers operation, finally bowing out on 5 April 1995. *Mark Darby*

Although numerically the second member of the 121 class of 'Small' GMs, No 122 actually became the ninth member to be placed into service, on 4 March 1961. During the balmy summer evening of 16 August 1993, No 122 passes over the tidal estuary of the River Nanny, propelling a Mark 3 push-pull set forming the 17.07 Drogheda to Dublin Pearse service away from Laytown station, which opened to traffic on 25 May 1844. Laytown is well known for horse-racing along the beach, which takes place during June each year. Together with Nos 121, 125, 126, 130 and 132, No 122 officially suffered withdrawal on 24 July 2002 – a black day indeed for the class. *Antony Guppy*

On 19 October 2004 No 213 *Abhainn na Muaidhe/River Moy* sweeps past the site of Charleville Junction with the 12.00 North Wall-North Esk liner made up of air-braked container pocket wagons (CPWs). Until closure in 1967 the direct line to Limerick diverged here. The signal cabin closed in 1924 and, in a development that caused a sensation in the signalling world, the points and signals were converted to remote power operation from a hand generator in Charleville cabin, more than a mile away. The CPWs were built with EU support by Talgo OY of Finland to take a 10-foot-high container. IÉ discontinued the carriage of individual containers in July 2005 and, in a development that caused a sensation in the enthusiast world, the CPWs became redundant after seeing less than three years of service. No more need be said.
Paul Quinlan

No 144 ambles through the delightful wayside halt of Cloughjordan, at the head of the Nenagh branch bagged cement train returning from Roscrea to Mungret cement factory on 19 May 1997. Starting in 1976, 172 of these 20-ton wagons were turned out from Inchicore. Painted in the house colours of Irish Cement, they became known as 'blues'. Their highly innovative design used pulleys and counterweights to vertically open the full-length bodyside doors. Ingeniously, this gave unrestricted access for quick and efficient mechanised handling of the palletised product, allowing small depots like Roscrea to function with no more than a concrete apron, a forklift and a covered store. From the mid-1990s curtain sides began to replace the steel doors, being simpler and cheaper to maintain, and both variants are seen here. Roscrea closed for bagged cement in 1997, soon followed by Nenagh, so the Nenagh branch cement traffic passed into history. During the summer of 2003, in the midst of the construction boom, IÉ ceased to carry bagged cement by rail and scrapped the remaining 'blues'. Although it had closed as a block post 30 years previously, the signal cabin on the left is still in remarkably good condition, and happily, as this was written in April 2009, No 144 is still with us. *Aidan McDonnell*

The distinctive-looking Cravens were built by Cravens Ltd of Sheffield and CIÉ's Inchicore Works. The first of the vacuum-braked fleet, which eventually totalled 55 vehicles, entered revenue service in 1964. Over the ensuing 42 years the arrival of newer stock progressively cascaded them from premier Cork expresses down to branch trains and Friday-only workings. On the beautiful morning of Thursday 14 September 2006, Nos 124 and 134 power around the long gentle curve near Kyle

Crossing hauling six Cravens and four BR vans on their last journey, to Inchicore, where they are to be quickly scrapped. They had been stored in Cork for many months, where they had been easy prey for the vandals, as can be seen from the many broken windows. The Cravens finally bowed out on 11 December 2006, the 05.15 Athlone-Heuston service bringing the steam heat era to an end on IÉ. *Paul Quinlan*

No 210 *Abhainn na Heirne/River Erne* shunts the cement terminal at Cork on 26 July 1995 after arrival from Limerick Castlemungret cement works. Less than a year old and adorned in the original orange and black livery, No 210 would have been truly a mixed-traffic loco at this time, found on both passenger and freight. Designated by GM as a JT42HCW, these Ontario-built locos were the first to feature the 3,200hp V12 EMD 7103B engine. Little did people realise that the 'ying-ying' of the engine would soon become very common in the UK, as this prime mover is the same as that fitted to UK Class 66 and 67 locos, as is the loco's 'brain', the EM2000 traction computer. *Neil Higson*

On 2 May 2008 No 225 *Abhainn na Daoile/River Deel* powers the 14.35 Dublin Heuston to Galway service away from Portarlington, wearing its smart new 'InterCity' livery, a colour scheme that was first seen on No 228 back in December 2005 and now adorns most of the push-pull-fitted locos. Its nine orange and black Derby-built Mark 3 coaches, most of which now have an uncertain future, were built between 1984 and 1985, being based on the similar British Rail Mark 3s except for a few detail differences, such as plug doors and the 2+2 table seating, which perhaps a few UK TOCs ought to come and sample!
Neil Higson

The sole named 'Big' GM, No 082 *Cumann Na nInnealtoiri* (*The Institution of Engineers of Ireland*) shatters the silence of County Wexford at Ballynahallin, between Gorey and Enniscorthy, with the 14.45 Rosslare Europort to Dublin Connolly service on 14 August 2000. At the time of the photograph, members of the ILDA (Irish Locomotive Drivers Association) were involved in industrial action, with many services affected as the strike had already been running for almost two months. In the west of the country, the Mayo branch was one of the worst affected lines. A separate threatened strike by the line-workers' union was averted at a mammoth meeting in a Dublin hotel at 05.00 on the day this picture was taken. If the withdrawal of labour had proceeded, the whole network would have ground to a halt within two days. *Mark Darby*

The diminutive wooden-bodied Park Royal coaches were part of the everyday scene for many years. On 28 April 1989 a train of the distinctive coaches arrives at Rush & Lusk behind 'Small' GM No 167, forming a Pearse to Drogheda suburban service. Containing no more than 11 levers, the signal cabin at Rush & Lusk was one of the smallest on the route. The signals behind the train, including the up starter, which is on the wrong side of the line, disappeared on 16 May 1994 when the Malahide to Drogheda section was resignalled for CTC. *Colm O'Callaghan*

Working K202, the Marino Point to Shelton Abbey ammonia tanks, No 039 trundles past the Irish Sea south of Greystones on 1 July 1993. This popular train started running on 25 July 1979 utilising a fleet of 20 wagons built by French company Fauvet-Girel. Each day for more than 23 years three six-wagon, 530-tonne trains, which also incorporated water-filled barrier wagons at each end for use in emergencies, supplied the Shelton Abbey IFI plant. Trials were conducted using a 'River' class loco and nine lpg wagons on a two-trains-per-day basis during the mid-1990s, but they were quietly dropped after a number of months, reverting to the standard formation. *Douglas Johnson*

On 5 April 1996 a rake of Mark 2 air-braked stock, known Republic-wide as the "LIMA" coaches, make a highly unusual sortie along the erstwhile DSER route, substituting for the Mk 2ds, which were principal fare of the time. Forming the 13.38 Dublin Connolly to Rosslare Harbour service, No 076 eases the train over the River Slaney after the booked stop at Enniscorthy. Sadly, Rosslare services succumbed to the inevitable, when Class 2700 'Arrow' railcars took over on Monday 26 July 2004. The former British Rail Mk 2s would more commonly have been found operating over the routes to Limerick, Waterford or Ballina. 'River' class No 212 is the bearer of the name *River Slaney*, although it is doubtful it will ever see the river at Enniscorthy, as the class is officially barred between Arklow and Wellington Bridge except in 'emergencies', the only recorded working (under power) within the restricted section of line being No 227 with a 'cement' on 17 September 2004. *Dave Brush*

No 185 creates a perfect reflection in the still waters below as it creeps across the River Barrow on 20 September 2002. It has just started its journey back to Limerick with the empty cement tanks from the Tegral building materials factory in Athy, situated on the river bank behind the train. This short spur is all that remains of the Wolfhill branch, opened in 1918 to tap coal deposits during the shortages of the First World War. The rails and sleepers were obtained by singling the Athy-Carlow section. The Athy 'cement' would continue until March 2005, when it fell victim to the relentless withdrawal from rail freight. *Paul Quinlan*

In 1995 the Iarnród Éireann timetable advertised selected services on the routes to Cork, Limerick and Tralee under the branding 'City Gold', which afforded the passenger the highest-quality 'ultimate experience' of train travel. The 21st-century rail service boasted personal catering together with on-board use of phone and fax! 'City Gold' is rather apt for this image. Although not on a line to benefit from 'personal service' and mod cons, No 087 prepares for departure from Dublin Connolly at the head of the 18.30 service for Rosslare Harbour on 6 October 1995. That autumn day experienced much inclement weather; however, as evening approached, the clouds parted to highlight the train in a golden hue! The large dome, picked out by the shadows behind the locomotive's cab, houses part of the auxiliary generator. *Mark Darby*

On a rather glorious 4 June 2007, 201-class No 202 *Abhainn na Laoi/River Lee* heads through the hamlet of Cuiskell hauling a rake of Mark 3s a few minutes into its 161-mile journey as the 13.10 service from Westport to Dublin Heuston. The magnificent distinctive mountain in the background is Croagh Patrick – with an elevation of more than 2,500 feet, it is as fascinating as it is high. It is said that in 441 AD Ireland's patron saint, Saint Patrick, spent 40 days on the slopes praying for the Irish! It is also rumoured to contain deposits of gold, and furthermore, should one ascend to the peak to witness the beautiful panoramic views afforded of Clew Bay, one may attempt to count all 365 islands visible – an island for every day of the year! *Mark Few*

Barrack Street in Dundalk was originally the terminus of the Dundalk & Enniskillen Railway, but downgrading to a freight yard eventually followed. On 12 April 1994 a pair of 'Small' GMs are captured on film beneath the overhead crane shunting the 15.10 container train from Belfast Adelaide. Barrack Street closed at the end of March 1995 with freight handling transferred over to Ardee Road, which opened for business on the 27th of the same month. The two GMs illustrated are no longer with us, Nos 183 and 165 being scrapped in September 2006 and August 2008 respectively. *Antony Guppy*

No 233 *Abhainn na Chlair/River Clare*, with the Marino Point to Shelton Abbey ammonia tanks, skirts the Irish Sea on arguably the most scenic stretch of railway in Ireland, the section that snakes between Bray and Greystones, designed by Isambard Kingdom Brunel in 1855. Unfortunately, the coastal route has suffered extensive erosion and has been rebuilt several times, gaining the name 'Brunel's Folly' in the process. The disused tunnel in the background is part of the abandoned route. Since this shot was taken on 24 July 1995, electrification masts have spoiled the view somewhat. *Neil Higson*

On Monday 28 May 2001 the weed-spray train traversed the Nenagh branch from Limerick to Ballybrophy and back. Seen here on the outward journey, No 152 trundles slowly past the village of Borris in Ossory, a few miles from 'Bally'. The train is in the charge of guard Dom Donovan and driver Eamon Jones from Portlaoise depot, two of life's thorough gentlemen, who worked on it frequently. The sprayer was usually crewed by Portlaoise men, who maintained system-wide route knowledge because of their work on trains to all parts of the country from IÉ's main permanent way depot there. In April 2007 this venerable collection of vehicles was replaced by a new spray train, featuring former BR van 3187 as the spray van and utilising spare bogie flats in place of the two-axle wagons seen here. *Paul Quinlan*

Left: Working a laden beet train from Wellington Bridge to Mallow on Saturday 21 October 2000, Nos 157 and 154 run along the banks of the River Suir. They have just passed Belview Port, and are approaching Abbey Junction, Waterford. The South Wexford line from Rosslare Strand to Abbey Junction was built to realise the ambitions of the GWR to open a new route between Britain and Ireland and secure for itself a larger share of the traffic from the south and south-west of the country, to be delivered onto GWR metals via the short sea crossing from Rosslare Harbour to Fishguard. Once host to the famed Rosslare-Cork boat expresses, by 2000 it had a very poor 'service' of only two return passenger trains per day, and a few Norfolk liners for Belview, augmented by heavy traffic during the three-month beet season. In 2002 the IÉ Board decided to suspend services on the line from Rosslare Strand through to Limerick Junction, and put the line on 'care and maintenance' – in other words, closure. It was saved by the intervention of the Minister for Transport following a public outcry, and agitation by the powerful Irish Farmers Association on behalf of the local beet growers. Now that the beet is gone, will the few passenger trains and the 'Norfolks' be enough to keep this line open? *Paul Quinlan*

Opposite: No 081 makes a fine sight passing Kilberry near Athy with the colourful 12.00 Ballina to Waterford 'Norfolk' on 29 April 2007. On arrival at Waterford Belview docks the containers will be unloaded from the 18 wagons and transhipped to a Norfolk Line container ship before embarking on the 35-hour trip to Rotterdam in Holland. An impressive way to move goods to Europe, it almost seems criminal that opportunities like this have been thrown away with the withdrawal of so many container services in Ireland. With so much talk of 'carbon footprints', why do governments sit back and allow this to happen? Short-term profits is the likely answer. *Neil Higson*

For anyone who has ever been fortunate enough to enjoy the fabulous sound produced by an 071 class locomotive in full cry at close quarters, this powerful photograph epitomises the experience. With the 150-foot-high spire of the Church of the Assumption forming an imposing backdrop, No 073 pounds away from Collooney, making good time with A907, the 18.15 Sligo to Dublin Connolly service, on 23 May 1996. During St Stephen's Day two years after this image was recorded, winds gusting at 120mph removed five courses of the church's masonry and a much-loved bronze cross. Collooney remains the truncated junction of the 'Burma Road' from Claremorris. A constant and very obvious groundswell of local and national opinion continues with its aim of reinstating this once important rail corridor linking Limerick with Sligo. *Antony Guppy*

Yet to acquire 'dayglo' orange warning panels, No 026 pauses in the loop at Navan on 9 May 1994 with M105, the 10.20 Tara Mines to Alexandra Road train. For some reason best known to the operating department, No 026 swapped with No 036, the locomotive that arrived at the head of the M102 empties from Dublin. The zinc concentrate from Tara is presently exported to the smelters at Kokkola in Finland and Odda in Norway. Navan closed as a station way back in 1958; however, the Transport 21 policy document of November 2005 advocated its reopening, together with three other suburban lines, and also proposed electrification. *Mark Darby*

On the clearest of days it is possible to see Wales across the Irish Sea from the top of Killiney Hill on the Irish Riviera! This August 1973 view portrays a morning Bray to Dublin service approaching Dalkey Tunnel. The train is being propelled by an unidentified B201 class locomotive, with control car No 6106 leading the former AEC railcar stock. No 6106, formerly numbered 2634, was converted into push-pull stock at Inchicore in 1973; withdrawal came in 1984, and it was subsequently scrapped at Mullingar. *Richard Wall*

On 2 May 2008 No 073, in ex-works condition, powers the 17.10 Dublin to Athlone service through the popular location of Sallins, near Naas, on the westbound main line out of Dublin. All Galway, Westport, Cork, Waterford and Limerick services pass through here, producing up to 10 loco-hauled trains in just a few hours during the rush hour before the invasion of the Class 22000 units.

No 081 was the first to be painted in this distinctive black and silver 'freight' livery in March 2007 at Inchicore, and by February 2008 it had been applied to eight locomotives, hopefully indicating their long-term future use. *Neil Higson*

This image shows a 'Small' GM going about one of the duties synonymous with the class for many years, and one that the final survivors still perform today – the Dublin Heuston station pilot. On 21 January 1999 No 149 has been diagrammed for this role and is seen dragging Inchicore-built (1987-8) composite No 7169 out of the carriage maintenance shed after some remedial work. Introduced into traffic in December 1962, No 149 lasted in service for more than 45 years until withdrawal in the summer of 2008 – phenomenal value for money! *Mark Darby*

No 186 has cleared the summit of the long climb up out of Clonmel with six bogies of containers and 20 'bubbles' forming the 11.34 Waterford-Limerick empty cement train on Saturday 27 September 2003. Behind the train the crossing-keeper is already opening Nicholastown gates for road traffic – these were due to be swept away by modern CCTV barriers in 2009. No 186 was involved in a serious derailment a few miles from Claremorris on Sunday 24 September 1989. While leading No 177 on the 07.30 Balbriggan-Claremorris 'Knock Special', the train struck a herd of cattle that were, rather incredibly, being herded along the line by a local farmer. Although the coaches were badly damaged, some ending up on their sides, thankfully there were no fatalities among the 450 or so passengers and crew, but around 80 of them were hospitalised. Having been stripped for parts earlier in 2006, No 186 succumbed to the cutter's torch at Inchicore in the week ending 16 September. *Paul Quinlan*

Formed by two Cravens and a brake generating steam van, 'Small' GM No 164 saunters past the former station at Ballyvary on 24 May 1996, forming the 18.20 service from Ballina to Manulla Junction; on arrival at the latter station at 18.51, it will provide a booked connection with the 18.30 Westport to Dublin service. The 'Small' GM will then follow the express with the empty stock, to stable it at Claremorris. The attractive former station building behind the train, which closed on 17 June 1963, is currently a private residence. No 164 was reduced to scrap during February 2005. *Antony Guppy*

Running to time along the north bank of the River Suir, No 077 snakes her way over the pointwork as she approaches journey's end with A504, the down 11.40 service from Dublin Heuston, on 12 July 1995. A short distance beyond the final coach lies Waterford West, at the time a block post, and the former junction for the direct main route through to Mallow via Dungarvan, which closed to passenger traffic in 1967. Twenty-six miles of the route remained to serve Quigleys Magnesite plant until its untimely demise at the end of July 1982. The branch remained part of the national network for more than a decade afterwards, when the span bridging the River Suir was removed. Although famous for the world's finest-quality cut crystal, Waterford also boasts a proud maritime pedigree, being a deep-water harbour lying at the mouth of three rivers, the Nore, Barrow and Suir, which are collectively known as the 'three sisters'. *Mark Darby*

In the final few days of the 2000 beet campaign, Nos 163 and 167 thread their way cautiously through a freezing Tipperary on Friday 29 December, with empty beet wagons destined for Wellington Bridge. Although nominally a 10.39 Mallow-Waterford light engine move, it was often a convenient way to get empties back to Wellington Bridge. While the returning empties could load up to 36 wagons and were allowed to travel at 40mph, laden trains were limited to 25 wagons weighing 775 tonnes, and were restricted to 35mph. At the sugar factory, the 500-tonne payload was removed by opening the doors and hosing the beet out of the wagons using high-pressure water jets. In a demonstration of the enthusiasm with which surplus motive power is now eliminated, No 163 met a swift end. It was happily shunting at Inchicore on 13 December 2008 but, with the financial year-end beckoning, a mere four days later it had been reduced to scrap metal. *Paul Quinlan*

Having crossed the 15.25 Limerick-Rosslare passenger, and with engines growling, Nos 157 and 154 ease out of the loop at Tipperary on Thursday 19 October 2000, heading for Mallow sugar factory with a laden beet train. From its opening in September 1979, nearly all trains from the Central Beet Loading Depot at Wellington Bridge went to Thurles sugar factory, although some went to Tuam. From 1985 Wellington Bridge became the last station to load beet, and when Thurles closed after the 1988 beet campaign, the trains were diverted to Mallow from the start of the following year's season. As it had last received beet by rail about 15 years previously, the factory yard there was removed and rebuilt with redundant track panels recovered from the Thurles factory. No 157 still carries the original marker lights that it bore when it was delivered in 1962, while No 154 has the new LED markers that were first trialled on No 130 in 1999. Bigger, brighter and cheaper to maintain, they subsequently became widespread across the rest of the loco fleet. Nos 157 and 154 were scrapped at Inchicore in February 2005 and June 2007 respectively. *Paul Quinlan*

No 078 stands silent at the Tullamore Irish Cement siding on 30 April 2008 waiting for a driver to return it to Platin early the next morning, having arrived at 10.13 that morning as service N822 from Dublin North Wall. This service restarted after a few years of non-activity on Tuesday 25 March 2008 when No 086 and 20 of the distinctive four-wheel 'bubbles' arrived at the county town of Offaly. One hundred and fifty of these popular wagons were built in seven batches between 1964 and 1972, with later batches painted in CIÉ orange tan, but this has been lost after many years of cement spillage! *Neil Higson*

The last rays of winter sun give a warming glow to No 148 leading its train of 'bubbles' through Lisduff, forming the 12.40 empty cement train from Athy to Limerick at 15.57 on 7 November 2003. The 14.25 Cork-Heuston service is racing away in the opposite direction, powered by No 209. To the right lies Lisduff Hill; composed of solid limestone, from about 1907 its quarry supplied high-quality stone to the railway, becoming the main source of ballast for CIÉ. When the quality of the stone deteriorated and was no longer suitable, Irish Rail closed the quarry in 1993. The remaining conveyors are visible through the trees. A ballast train stands in the yard, which remains in use for loading stone that is now brought in by road. No 148 met its end at Inchicore in September 2006. *Paul Quinlan*

When the revamped Dublin-Belfast 'Enterprise' service was launched in 1997, a striking new livery was devised for the brand-new HEP-equipped De Dietrich carriages that had been dedicated to the service. Locos Nos 206-209 were repainted to match, the intention being that they would be similarly dedicated. In practice, to provide a respite from the ferocious demands that HEP imposes upon them, they can often be found wandering the system far from their intended stamping grounds. Fire was a contributing factor to No 206 *Abhainn na Life/River Liffey* being out of traffic with serious alternator damage from May 2003 to May 2005, but 11 months on and all is well, as on Sunday 23 April 2006 the 'Enterprise'-liveried loco is captured on film in north County Cork. Motoring along near Buttevant with a 07.50 Cork-Heuston special, it is taking Munster Rugby supporters to the Heineken Cup semi-final against arch-rivals Leinster. Munster won the match with a scoreline of 30-6, securing their place in the final at the Millennium Stadium, Cardiff. After a heart-stopping game that held the entire country spellbound, Munster eventually emerged victorious over mighty Biarritz by 23-19, to become European Champions for the first time. *Paul Quinlan*

With a cab door open to let in some air on the hot afternoon of 5 July 2001, No 164 is working hard with a laden shale train as it accelerates away from Birdhill, having slowed to collect the staff for Killonan Junction. Shale is a sedimentary rock used as one of the main raw materials in the manufacture of cement. This traffic started in 1982 from the nearby siding at Kilmastulla, the air-braked wagons being specially built at Inchicore for the 20-mile trip to the Irish Cement factory at Mungret on the outskirts of Limerick. No 164 would be scrapped at Inchicore in February 2005. *Paul Quinlan*

No 222 *Abhainn na Dargaile/River Dargle* drops down the link towards Cherryville Junction with the 15.05 Dublin to Waterford Mark 3 service on 29 April 2008. Cherryville Junction is situated 32 miles from Dublin and since 1976 has been signalled from the CTC Centre at Dublin Connolly station. On the evening of 21 August 1983 the junction was the location of a fatal accident when the 18.50 Galway to Dublin Heuston service hauled by No 086 crashed into the back of the 17.15 Tralee to Dublin Heuston, hauled by No 009. Sadly, seven people were killed and 55 injured, not helped by four 1950s-vintage wooden-bodied coaches in the consist of the Tralee train, one of which was completely destroyed. *Neil Higson*

No 071, the first member of its 21-strong class, was introduced into service on 30 May 1977 and helped displace the 'A' class locomotives. On 29 April 2008, 31 years later, it is seen in the new 2007 freight livery of yellow and black just south of Drogheda at Pilltown Bye Road, working the daily 12.00 Irish Cement flow from Platin to Dublin North Wall. It will then be sent to either Cork or Tullamore in the early hours of the next day. The 20 four-wheel 'bubbles' are restricted to 35mph, making their passage across the system more and more difficult as time passes. *Mark Davies*

Gormanston is the location as No 233 *Abhainn na Chlair/River Clare* and its eight coaches race north to Belfast with the 16.50 service from Dublin Connolly. 'Enterprise', the brand name of the cross-border inter-city train service, can be traced back to 1947 when the Great Northern Railway introduced an express service to compete with road transport. The current set-up commenced in September 1997 when new coaching stock built by the De Dietrich company in Reichshoffen, France, was introduced. Twenty-eight coaches based on the British Class 373 'Eurostar' concept were built, including four DVTs. They are formed into three sets of coaches and maintained by Translink at York Road, Belfast, with the six dedicated Class 201 locomotives coming under the control of IÉ at Inchicore. An unusual arrangement is that the odd-numbered coaches are owned by IÉ and the even numbers by NIR! As for the six locos, three different variants of livery have been applied, with NIR No 8208 now wearing a new coat of paint to match the coaching stock. *Neil Higson*

No volume covering traction on the Republic's metals would be complete without reference to the three push-pull-equipped NIR 101 DL class locomotives. Introduced in July 1970 for upgraded cross-border services, the 80mph machines were designed by Hunslet of Leeds, with assembly contracted out to British Rail Engineering Ltd at Doncaster. This sublime nostalgic view, dating from 1975, depicts No 101 *Eagle* in original maroon livery approaching Cement Factory Junction, north of Drogheda, heading the 14.30 Belfast Great Victoria Street to Dublin Connolly service. Another class member tails the formation. In 1978 NIR blue livery was applied to the class, but the arrival of the 111s in the early 1980s committed the entire class to more menial duties. On the right No A20r waits to come off the branch line with a train of empty gypsum and laden bagged cement vans from Boyne Road cement plant. Visible in the background, above the rear of the freight train, can be seen part of the aerial ropeway that conveyed limestone in suspended 'buckets' to the factory. Bagged products ceased around 1976, with the introduction of a new palletised wagon fleet. *Richard Wall*

On the afternoon of 15 April 1994 No 113 *Belfast and County Down* heads for the Republic with the mid-afternoon 'Enterprise'. Service A135, the 15.00 Belfast Central to Dublin Connolly, has just passed the former GNR(I) signal cabin at Poyntzpass, visible behind the train. This rural box survived for long enough to claim the honour of being the final example in use on the NIR system. At the time it boasted a 24-lever frame, containing 'bespoke' block instrumentation manufactured by both Tyers and Harper. On 17 November 1996 the signal cabin closed, with control passing to the panel at Portadown. *Antony Guppy*

Representing a 'River' class loco in Northern Irish Railways' attractive blue livery, No 208 makes for the border as she threads the cutting in Fathom Park, to the south of Newry, with the mid-afternoon 'Enterprise', the 15.00 Belfast Central to Dublin Connolly service, on 12 April 1997. At the time of the photograph the Canadian GM was only a couple of years old, and had yet to receive its *River Lagan* nameplates.
Antony Guppy

The attractive Drumbanagher church, which provides a rather pleasing foreground, was built around 1840, and is frequently commented on by passengers as they pass through the rolling countryside at Jerrettspass, to the north of Newry. On a glorious 16 April 1994 No 112 *Northern Counties* has charge of A141, the 17.00 Belfast Central to Dublin Connolly 'Enterprise' service.

The first two of the three 111-class locomotives were not placed into traffic until February 1981, almost four years after their cousins south of the border. Only their livery and the cab-to-shore communications systems set the 071s and 111s apart. *Antony Guppy*

Any traveller who has ever taken a trip to the Emerald Isle will be more than aware that the sun always shines; however, to redress this popularly held belief it was deemed necessary to include a portrayal of the opposing view! Battling through torrential rain, No 202 *Abhainn na Laoi/River Lee* clears the west-end pointwork at Geashill with the 16.05 Sundays-only Dublin Heuston to Galway service, beautifully captured by photographer Antony Guppy in this atmospheric image from 27 April 2008. The twin red tail lights, which became mandatory after the Cherryville Junction accident of 21 August 1983, shine beacon-like through the inclement conditions. Closed as a station as far back as 17 June 1963, Geashill passing loop is located midway between Portarlington and Tullamore. *Antony Guppy*